SRA
Reading
Mastery®
Transformations

Language Arts
Textbook

Siegfried Engelmann

Bonnie Grossen

Steve Osborn

Jerry Silbert

Mc
Graw
Hill

Acknowledgments

The authors are grateful to the following people for their assistance in the preparation of manuscript for Reading Mastery 4: Debbi Kleppen and Cally Dwyer.

PHOTO CREDITS

13 (tl)McGraw-Hill Education, (tc)McGraw-Hill Companies Inc./Ken Karp, photographer, (bc)Big Cheese Photo/SuperStock; **18** (tl)Photo by Keith Weller, USDA-ARS, (tr)Pixtal/age fotostock; **45** (tl)McGraw-Hill Education, (tr)McGraw-Hill Education, (bc)McGraw-Hill Education; **47** McGraw-Hill Education, (tl)McGraw-Hill Education; **49** (tl)McGraw-Hill Education, (tr)McGraw-Hill Education; **51** McGraw-Hill Education, (tc) McGraw-Hill Education, (tr)McGraw-Hill Education; **89** (tl)J.D. Griggs/USGS, (tr)Jim Vallance/USGS; **131** (bl) Photo by Ela2007/Getty Images, (br)McGraw-Hill Education; **148** (b)Loretta Hostettler/Getty Images; **158** (cr)Stefan Sollfors/Alamy; **245** (b)Getty Images/Moment Open; **246** (b)MPI/Archive Photos/Getty Images.

mheducation.com/prek-12

Copyright © 2021 McGraw-Hill Education

Send all inquiries to:
McGraw-Hill Education
8787 Orion Place
Columbus, OH 43240

ISBN: 978-0-07-905539-2
MHID: 0-07-905539-7

Printed in the United States of America.

2 3 4 5 6 7 8 9 10 LWI 26 25 24 23 22 21

A INTRODUCTION

- Write well
- Think clearly
- Understand details of sentences
- People who don't think clearly are easily fooled
- Better at finding inaccuracies and misleading claims
- Organize information
- Punctuate sentences
- Express ideas clearly

B ORALLY IDENTIFY SUBJECT AND PREDICATE

The subject

Names

The predicate

Tells more

1. The boys were happy.

2. Those little boys were happy.

3. Those little boys on the playground were happy.

4. Those little boys on the playground threw stones in the air.

5. Five boys threw stones.

6. They threw large stones.

7. Their mothers became angry.

8. The mothers told the boys to stop.

A good way to explain some things is with parallel sentences.

Here's a pair of parallel sentences:

> **They fed sheep.**
> **They also fed goats.**

Here's another pair of parallel sentences:

> **Their house was big.**
> **Their garage was also big.**

You're going to write parallel sentences that have the word **also.**

They did their math homework.

D **For each item, write a parallel sentence with the word _also_.**

1. They cut down a large tree. 2. She wore a blue blouse. 3. The walls are dirty.

4. Squirrels were on the roof. 5. The dog was under the table.

The people carried a chair.

The people wore pants.

The people moved from a house.

2. Two people

4. Her husband

3. The woman

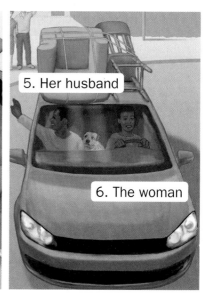

5. Her husband

6. The woman

| carried | tied | put | drove |
| waved | chair | rope | neighbors |

Check M: Does each sentence report on the main thing the person did?

Check SP: Does each sentence have a subject and a predicate?

Check CP: Does each sentence begin with a capital and end with a period?

☐ **M**   ☐ **SP**   ☐ **CP**

END OF LESSON 1

A IDENTIFY NOUN AND VERB

Here are rules for identifying some parts of speech in most simple sentences:

Rule 1: The last word of the subject is a **noun.**

Rule 2: The first word of the predicate is a **verb.**

B For each item, write a parallel sentence with the word *also*.

1. The girl's father was happy.

2. The man brushed his teeth.

3. She carried a box.

4. They had red paint.

5. A cat was in the garden.

The children picked up a little bird.

The children saved a little bird.

The children found a little bird.

2. A little bird

3. James

4. His sister

5. James

6. She

| bird | helped | fell | nest |
| ground | climbed | tree | branch |

Check M: Does each sentence report on the main thing the person did?

Check SP: Does each sentence have a subject and a predicate?

Check CP: Does each sentence begin with a capital and end with a period?

▢ **M**   ▢ **SP**   ▢ **CP**

END OF LESSON 2

3

A Write parallel statements that use the word *also*.

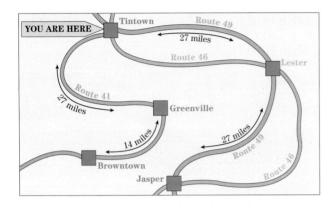

1. You can get to Greenville on Route 41.
   You can [____] get to [_____] on Route 41.

2. You can get to Lester on route 49.
   You can [____] get to [_____] on Route 49.
   You can [____] get to Lester on [____].

B NARRATIVE WRITING

A woman ran fast.

The woman saved a boy.

A woman saw a boy.

| threw | over | toward | street | brakes |
| tried | picked | grabbed | rolled | truck |

Check M: Does each sentence report on the main thing the person did?

Check SP: Does each sentence have a subject and a predicate?

Check CP: Does each sentence begin with a capital and end with a period?

☐ **M**   ☐ **SP**   ☐ **CP**

INDEPENDENT WORK

C For each item, write a parallel sentence with the word *also*.

1. She bought a soft drink.

2. The garage was on fire.

3. Four rabbits were in the garden.

4. Tom's shirt was soaked.

5. The Adams Building had a broken window.

END OF LESSON 3

A **Write parallel statements that use the word *also*.**

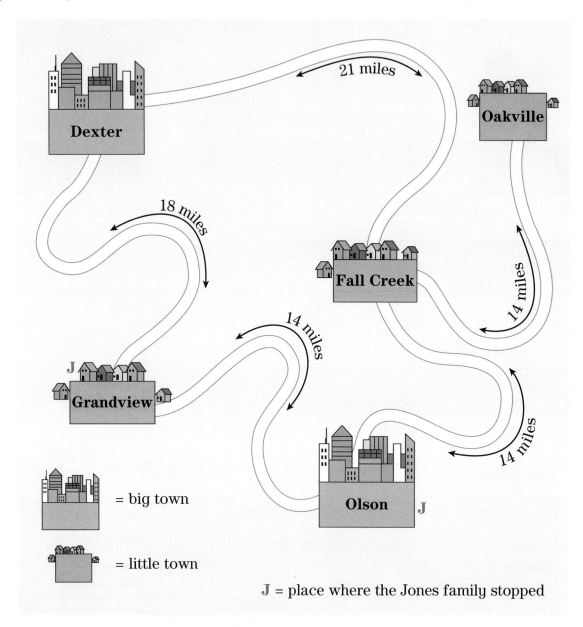

= big town

= little town

J = place where the Jones family stopped

1. Fall Creek is 14 miles from Olson.
   Fall Creek is also 14 miles from ▇▇▇▇ .

2. The Jones family stopped in a big town.
   ▇▇▇▇▇▇▇▇▇▇▇▇▇ .

3. The Jones family stopped 18 miles from Dexter.
   ▇▇▇▇▇▇▇▇▇▇▇ .

A girl prevented an accident.

wooden bridge	picture	painted	toward	lightning bolt
collapsed	burn	sign	driver	brakes

Check M: Does each sentence report on the main thing the person did?

Check SP: Does each sentence have a subject and a predicate?

Check CP: Does each sentence begin with a capital, end with a period and tell what happened?

☐ **M** ☐ **SP** ☐ **CP**

INDEPENDENT WORK

C For each statement, write a parallel sentence with the word *also*.

1. The girls wore sunglasses.

2. The students had tablets.

END OF LESSON 4

A INFORMATIVE TEXT

Icebergs

- 9/10 below surface
- often drift hundreds of miles

Check I: Did you explain each note clearly and accurately?

Check SP: Does each sentence have a subject and a predicate?

Check S: Did you correctly spell all the words that are given?

Check CP: Does each sentence begin with a capital and end with a period?

☐ **I**   ☐ **SP**   ☐ **S**   ☐ **CP**

INDEPENDENT WORK

B Write two parallel sentences for each item. Use the word *also* in one sentence.

1. She wore ▬▬▬▬▬ .

▬▬▬▬▬▬▬▬▬▬ .

2. ▬▬▬▬▬ in a tree.

▬▬▬▬▬▬▬▬▬▬ .

C If the sentence is not correct, rewrite it. Change the last underlined word.

1. <u>She</u> <u>like</u> to read romance stories.
2. <u>My</u> three <u>uncles</u> <u>puts</u> on a family picnic every summer.
3. The <u>bells</u> of that church <u>need</u> repair.
4. That little <u>kid</u> <u>spend</u> a lot of time talking.
5. <u>My</u> neighbor <u>own</u> dogs that bark a lot.

END OF LESSON 6

Greenland

- largest island
- glacier one mile thick
- parts of land below sea level

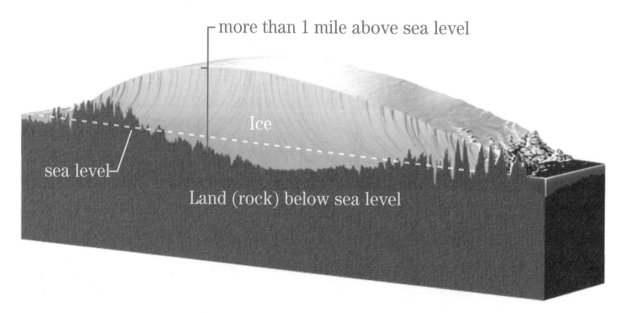

more than 1 mile above sea level

Ice

sea level

Land (rock) below sea level

Check I: Did you explain each note clearly and accurately?

Check NM: Does each sentence have a subject and a predicate?

Check S: Did you correctly spell all the words that are given?

Check CP: Does each sentence begin with a capital and end with a period?

☐ I   ☐ SP   ☐ S   ☐ CP

END OF LESSON 7

A USE QUOTATION MARKS FOR DIRECT SPEECH

Did you see my dog? It has big, brown spots.

We saw a good movie.

Tom

My friend

I ran 10 miles yesterday. How many miles did you run?

Alice

Greenland

- north of the Arctic Circle
- no sun in winter
- snow every month
- temperature almost always below freezing

Check I: Did you explain each note clearly and accurately?

Check SP: Does each sentence have a subject and a predicate?

Check S: Did you correctly spell all the words that are given?

Check CP: Does each sentence begin with a capital and end with a period?

☐ **I**   ☐ **SP**   ☐ **S**   ☐ **CP**

A Write a parallel sentence for each statement.

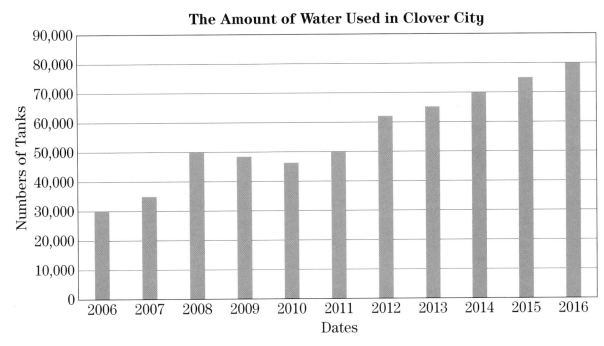

1. Clover City used 50,000 tanks of water in 2008.
2. Clover City used more than 65,000 tanks of water in 2014.
3. The amount of water decreased between 2008 and 2009.
4. Clover City used more than 50,000 tanks in 2012, 2013, and 2014.

Cumulonimbus Clouds

- 5 miles from top to bottom
- winds blow from bottom to top and back to bottom
- – 60 degrees at top
- + 70 degrees at bottom

Check I: Did you explain each note clearly and accurately?

Check SP: Does each sentence have a subject and a predicate?

Check S: Did you correctly spell all the words that are shown?

Check CP: Does each sentence begin with a capital and end with a period?

☐ **I**　　　　☐ **SP**　　　　☐ **S**　　　　☐ **CP**

END OF LESSON 9

A INFORMATIVE TEXT

Hailstones

- circle
- more than 100 mph
- freezes drops at top
- adds water at the bottom
- each ring = 1 circle
- the size of tennis balls

Vocabulary:	cumulonimbus	circle	droplets
	equals	hailstone	tennis

Check I: Did you explain each note clearly and accurately?

Check SP: Does each sentence have a subject and a predicate?

Check S: Did you correctly spell all the words that are given?

Check CP: Does each sentence begin with a capital and end with a period?

☐ I   ☐ SP   ☐ S   ☐ CP

When you write a parallel sentence, you use as many words as possible from the original sentence.

Here's a picture that shows animals raised on farms.

Here's a sentence: **Chickens are the only animals that are raised on farms.**

Here are parallel sentences that start with the word **no:**

No, cows are also raised on farms.

No, cows are also animals that are raised on farms.

The best parallel sentence is the sentence that uses the greatest number of words from the original sentence.

C

1. Write a parallel sentence that disagrees with the original. Start with the word No.

2. Then circle the subject, underline the predicate, write N above the noun and V above the verb.

Chickens are the only animals that are raised on the farm.

No, cows are also animals that are raised on the farm.

1. Dogs are the only domesticated animals that can be kept inside houses.
2. Ducks are the only birds you see near water.
3. The carrot is the only vegetable that is not all green.

END OF LESSON 10

A INFORMATIVE TEXT

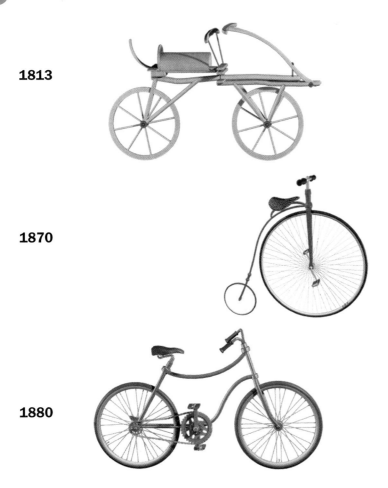

1813

1870

1880

Vocabulary: built appeared modern improvement

Notes:

- first bicycle—1813, run and coast
- pedals—1870
- chain—1880, tires filled with air

Check I: Did you explain each note clearly and accurately?

Check SP: Does each sentence have a subject and a predicate?

Check S: Did you correctly spell all the words that are shown?

Check CP: Does each sentence begin with a capital and end with a period?

☐ **I**   ☐ **SP**   ☐ **S**   ☐ **CP**

B **Write a parallel sentence for each item.**

> Only young men should work on construction crews.
> No, older men can also work on construction crews.

1.

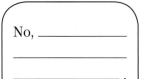

Candy is the only food that people should avoid eating before dinner.

No, _____ _____ _____ .

2.

Skydiving is the only sport that is dangerous.

_____ _____ _____ .

3.

Wood is the only important material used to build houses.

_____ _____ _____ .

END OF LESSON 11

A For each sentence, write a parallel sentence that uses *indicate*, *indicates*, or *indicated*.

- The word **indicate** means show or tell something.
- Here's a sentence: **The weather forecast told that a storm was on the way.**
- Here's a parallel sentence that uses a form of the word **indicate: The weather forecast indicated that a storm was on the way.**
- Remember, **indicate** means show or tell.

1. The map shows where the best parks are.
2. The shadows tell what time of day it is.
3. Their arguments showed that they wanted four recess periods.

B CONVEY IDEAS PRECISELY

Statements

1. Only girls go to school.
2. All adult birds can fly.
3. The first bicycle appeared before 1850.
4. Columbus landed in America before 1500.

Outline Diagram

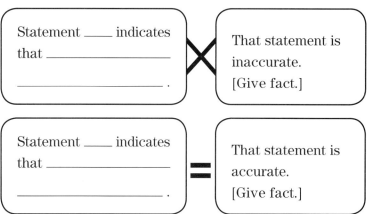

Check OD: Did you follow the **outline diagram** precisely?

Check S: Did you correctly **spell** all the words that are shown?

Check F: Did you write a **parallel fact** sentence that supports your conclusion?

☐ OD   ☐ S   ☐ F

END OF LESSON 12

A **Follow the X-box diagram and write a paragraph that tells about each item.**

Statements

1. All vehicles have wheels.
2. Water freezes when it is between 28° and 38° Fahrenheit.
3. Cows are the only farm animals that give milk.

Outline Diagram

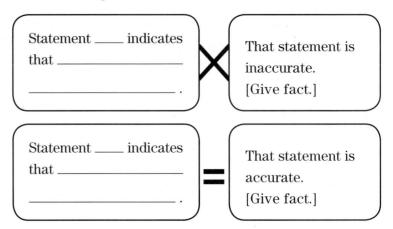

Check OD: Did you follow the **outline diagram** precisely?

Check S: Did you correctly **spell** all the words that are shown?

Check F: Did you write a **parallel fact** sentence that supports your conclusion?

☐ **OD**   ☐ **S**   ☐ **F**

B **Rewrite the underlined sentences so that the unclear word is clear.**

1. When Marco put the lid on the jar, it broke. He threw it out and covered the jar with tin foil.

2. Susan painted a picture of the elephant. It was enormous. When she hung it up, it covered the wall.

3. She made cookies for her children. They were small and sweet. The children waited patiently for them to cool.

4. When he put a bowl in the dishwasher, it broke. He pulled pieces of it from the dishwasher for weeks.

END OF LESSON 13

A Rewrite the underlined sentences so that the unclear word is clear.

1. They built a house in the meadow. <u>It was large and green.</u> The house stood right in the middle of it.

2. The radio interfered with her homework. <u>She threw it out the window.</u> On the next day, the teacher gave her 0 points for not turning in her assignment.

3. The bugs were getting in the peanuts. <u>I put them in the refrigerator.</u> Now I have cold bugs.

4. Two evil spies were after the letters Mr. Kelly wrote. <u>Mr. Kelly decided to destroy them.</u> They were made out of paper that burned easily.

B WRITE INFORMATIVE TEXT

Source

The moose is the largest member of the deer family. The adult male moose is called a bull. Bulls are about six feet tall and weigh about 1,400 pounds. They have a growth of skin called a *bell* that hangs from their neck. The bull's antlers may measure six feet in width. The bull's coat is not a single color. The bull's body is blackish brown. The bull's face, legs, and belly are light brown.

The cow's coat is a single light-brown color. The calves are also light brown all over. Calves are born in the spring. The principal diet of the moose during the winter consists of leaves and twigs.

Statements

1. A bull moose has a coat that is light brown all over.
2. The calf's coat resembles the cow's coat.

Outline Diagram

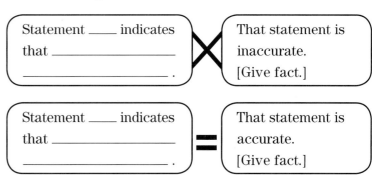

Statement _____ indicates that _____ _____ .

That statement is inaccurate. [Give fact.]

Statement _____ indicates that _____ _____ .

That statement is accurate. [Give fact.]

Check OD: Did you follow the **outline diagram** precisely?

Check S: Did you correctly **spell** all the words that are shown?

Check F: Did you write **parallel fact** sentences that support your conclusion?

☐ **OD**   ☐ **S**   ☐ **F**

END OF LESSON 14

A WRITE INFORMATIVE TEXT

Source

The moose is the largest member of the deer family. The adult male moose is called a bull. Bulls are about six feet tall and weigh about 1,400 pounds. They have a growth of skin called a *bell* that hangs from their neck. The bull's antlers may measure six feet in width. The bull's coat is not a single color. The bull's body is blackish brown. The bull's face, legs, and belly are light brown.

The cow's coat is a single light-brown color. The calves are also light brown all over. Calves are born in the spring. The principal diet of the moose during the winter consists of leaves and twigs.

Statements

1. The bull moose has very large antlers.
2. The winter diet of the moose consists of leaves and mushrooms.

Outline Diagram

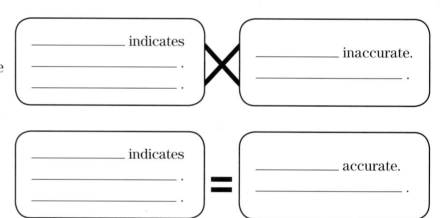

Check OD: Did you follow the **outline diagram** precisely?

Check S: Did you correctly **spell** all the words that are shown?

Check F: Did you write **parallel fact** sentences that support your conclusion?

☐ **OD**   ☐ **S**   ☐ **F**

B Rewrite the underlined sentences so that the unclear word is clear.

1. His children played with the dogs. <u>They loved to hide behind the couch.</u> The children searched all over for them.

2. Martina wanted to plant a rose in the window box. <u>Somebody stole it.</u> She put the rose in a large pot.

3. Farmer Jones gathered eggs from his chickens. <u>They were brown.</u> He gathered them from the chickens every morning.

END OF LESSON 15

A **Rewrite the underlined sentences so they are clear.**

1. Jack swung his bat at the ball. <u>It soared into space.</u> The coach said, "Don't let it slip out of your hands again."

2. Javier took a bus into the city. <u>It was crowded with holiday shoppers.</u> The streets were so crowded that Javier had trouble finding the things he wanted to buy.

3. He made a cake for the party. <u>It was a great success.</u> The rest of the party wasn't very good.

B **WRITE INFORMATIVE TEXT**

Source Map of Missouri River

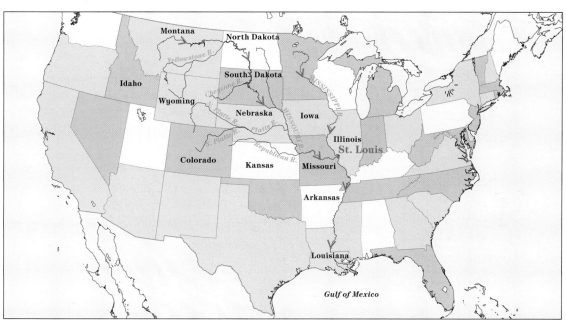

Statements **Outline Diagram**

1. The Missouri River ends at the Gulf of Mexico.

2. The Missouri River forms the east-west boundary between two states.

3. The Missouri River empties into another river.

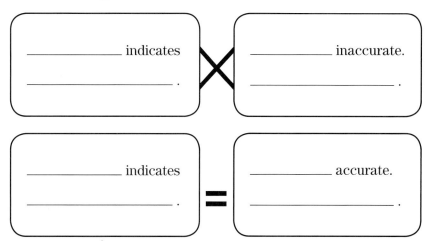

_____ indicates _____ inaccurate.
_____ . _____ .

_____ indicates _____ accurate.
_____ . _____ .

Check OD: Did you follow the **outline diagram** precisely?

Check S: Did you correctly **spell** all the words that are given?

Check F: Did you write **parallel fact** sentences that support your conclusion?

Check C: Did you **capitalize** the names of states and bodies of water?

☐ OD ☐ S ☐ F ☐ C

END OF LESSON 16

A Rewrite the underlined sentences so that the unclear word is clear.

1. <u>She put a potato in the oven, and it blew up.</u> Pieces of it were stuck all over the oven.

2. Sally ran into Rosa. <u>She started to cry.</u> Jason gave Rosa a tissue to wipe away her tears.

3. She set the cake on the table. <u>It collapsed.</u> She'll have to buy a new table.

B WRITE INFORMATIVE TEXT

Source: *Diagram of a Submarine*

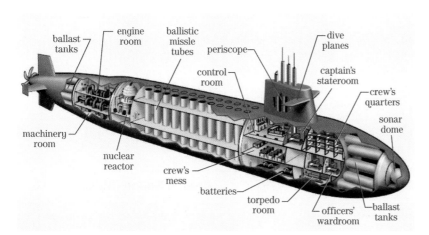

Statements

1. The place where the crew sleeps is in front of the place where the periscope is located.

2. The place where the crew eats is not on the same level as the captain's stateroom.

Definitions:

captain's stateroom—place where the captain sleeps

officers' wardroom—place where the officers eat and sleep

crew's quarters—place where the crew sleeps

crew's mess—place where the crew eats

Outline Diagram

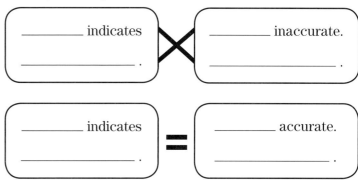

Check OD: Did you follow the **outline diagram** precisely?

Check S: Did you correctly **spell** all the words that are given?

Check F: Did you write **parallel fact** sentences that support your conclusion?

▪ **OD**   ▪ **S**   ▪ **F**

END OF LESSON 17

A WRITE INFORMATIVE TEXT

Source Data

Country	Population as of 2016	Area in Square Miles
Argentina	43,847,277	1,073,518
Bolivia	10,888,402	424,164
Brazil	209,567,920	3,287,597
Chile	18,131,850	291,930
Colombia	48,654,392	440,831
Ecuador	16,385,450	109,483
French Guiana	275,688	32,253
Guyana	770,610	83,000
Paraguay	6,725,430	157,048
Peru	31,774,225	496,225
Suriname	547,610	63,251
Uruguay	3,444,071	68,037
Venezuela	31,815,855	353,841
Total	424,465,186	6,881,178

Statements

1. Brazil is the largest country in South America.
2. Bolivia is the only country in South America that does not border the ocean.

Outline Diagram

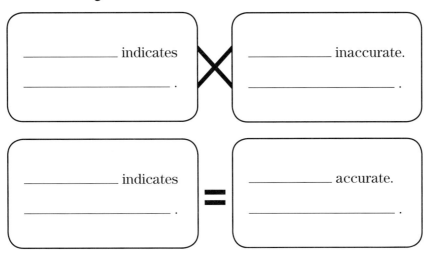

_____ indicates _____ .

_____ inaccurate _____ .

_____ indicates _____ .

_____ accurate _____ .

Check OD: Did you follow the **outline diagram** precisely?

Check S: Did you correctly **spell** all the words that are shown?

Check F: Did you write a **parallel fact** sentences that support your conclusion?

Check C: Did you **capitalize** the names of countries?

◼ OD   ◼ S   ◼ F   ◼ C

B **Rewrite the underlined sentences so that the unclear word is clear.**

1. As the sun rose over the desert, it turned pink. The desert is so beautiful when it is that color.

2. Tomas played violin in the orchestra. It produced lovely music. He didn't want to play any other violin.

3. We got to the pond by going through a wheat field. It was full of cows. Some of them were swimming.

END OF LESSON 18

A Rewrite the underlined sentences so that the unclear word is clear.

1. My dog won't bite that mail carrier. <u>He is friendly.</u> The only people that my dog bites are unfriendly.

2. We drove a truck in the parade. <u>It was full of clowns.</u> They kept falling out of the truck.

3. She put cheese on the bread. <u>She noticed that it was covered with mold.</u> She went to the store and bought some fresh bread.

B WRITE INFORMATIVE TEXT

Source Data

Country	Population as of 2016	Area in Square Miles
Argentina	43,847,277	1,073,518
Bolivia	10,888,402	424,164
Brazil	209,567,920	3,287,597
Chile	18,131,850	291,930
Colombia	48,654,392	440,831
Ecuador	16,385,450	109,483
French Guiana	275,688	32,253
Guyana	770,610	83,000
Paraguay	6,725,430	157,048
Peru	31,774,225	496,225
Suriname	547,610	63,251
Uruguay	3,444,071	68,037
Venezuela	31,815,855	353,841
Total	424,465,186	6,881,178

Statements

1. Chile is the only country in South America that borders two oceans.
2. Brazil touches the border of every other country in South America.
3. The population of French Guiana is less than 200,000.

Outline Diagram

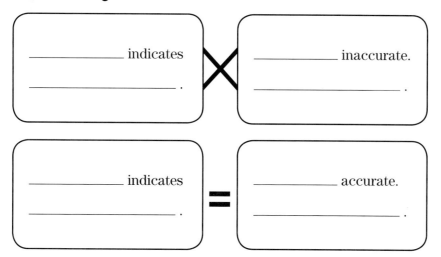

Check OD: Did you follow the **outline diagram** precisely?

Check S: Did you correctly **spell** all the words that are shown?

Check F: Did you write **parallel fact** sentences that support your conclusion?

Check C: Did you **capitalize** the names of countries?

▨ OD   ▨ S   ▨ F   ▨ C

END OF LESSON 19

A WRITE INFORMATIVE TEXT

Source Data

Softwood Species	Common Uses
Douglas Fir	piling, plywood, veneer, residential framing
Eastern White Pine	construction lumber, central layer of plywood paneling
Hemlock	containers, knotty paneling
Sugar pine	doors, frames, window blinds
Redwood	boards, joists, posts, outdoor furniture

Hardwood Species	Common Uses
Birch	cabinets, cupboards, plywood, veneer, doors
Black Cherry	furniture, caskets, fine veneer paneling
Mahogany	furniture, fine veneers, paneling
Red Oak	fence posts, truck floors
Teak	furniture, fine veneer paneling
Black Walnut	furniture, decorative paneling, cabinets

Statements

1. Douglas fir is commonly used for plywood.

2. Birch is commonly used for fence posts.

3. Black cherry and mahogany are the only woods used for paneling.

Outline Diagram

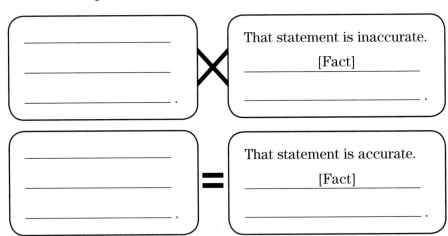

Check OD: Did you follow the **outline diagram** precisely?

Check S: Did you correctly **spell** all the words that are shown?

Check F: Did you write **parallel fact** sentences that support your conclusion?

☐ OD   ☐ S   ☐ F

INDEPENDENT WORK

B **Rewrite the underlined sentences so that the unclear word is clear.**

1. Peg saw the mountain from the lake. <u>It was beautiful.</u> The grass was brown and flat from the snow that had just melted, but the mountain was a crisp, jagged, white peak.
2. We saw Mike standing beside Phil. <u>He was wearing a red jacket.</u> Mike had on a blue jacket.

C **Write these sentences on your lined paper with as many contractions as you can make.**

1. Here is a new way to determine who is the winner.
2. You have no idea how much she does not like spinach.
3. He should not take the bus when it is so cold.

END OF LESSON 20

A   TRANSFORM COMPLETE SENTENCES

> ### Sample Sentence
>
> Three girls ate popcorn during the entire movie.
>
> During the entire movie, three girls ate popcorn.

1. A dog followed us as we went home.

2. The ground was soaked after the rainstorm.

B   Move part of the predicate to the front of the sentence and put a comma after it.

1. We will go home after finishing our work.
2. We caught a lot of fish at the pond.
3. He would buy a bike before the big race.
4. The campers sang songs as before.

INDEPENDENT WORK

C   Use the wording for either the X-box or Equal-box diagram to write a paragraph about each statement. Look up the boxed words in the Reference section if you don't know the fact.

Statements

1. Every fourth year is longer than 365 days.
2. The largest mammal is the elephant.
3. The tallest mountain in the world is over five miles high.

Outline Diagram

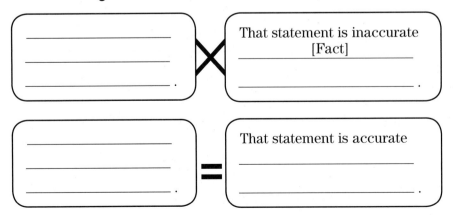

Check OD: Did you follow the **outline diagram** precisely?

Check S: Did you correctly **spell** all the words that are shown?

Check F: Did you write **parallel fact** sentences that support your conclusion?

    ☐ OD   ☐ S   ☐ F

END OF LESSON 21

A 1. **Rewrite each sentence so it begins with part of the predicate.**

2. **Circle the subject and underline the *whole* predicate, write <u>V</u> above the verb, <u>N</u> above the noun in the subject, or <u>P</u> above the pronoun.**

1. The last person left the meeting just before midnight.
2. My mom went to the store early in the morning.
3. Their cat walked along the ledge without looking down.
4. They may stop at the park after the picnic.

INDEPENDENT WORK

B **Use the wording for either the X-box or Equal-box diagram to write a paragraph about each statement. Look up the boxed words in the Reference Section if you don't know the fact.**

Statements

1. The great ⟨redwood⟩ forests are in Nebraska.
2. A ⟨corn⟩ plant has both male and female flowers.

Outline Diagram

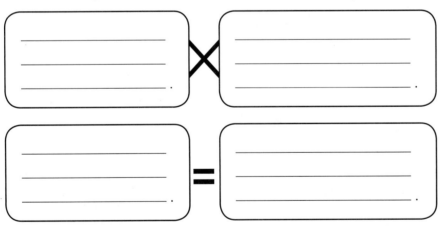

Check OD: Did you follow the **outline diagram** precisely?

Check S: Did you correctly **spell** all the words that are shown?

Check F: Did you write **parallel fact** sentences that support your conclusion?

☐ OD   ☐ S   ☐ F

A   **Rewrite the passage so that all the sentences are correct.**

Ana wanted to give her brother a guitar for his birthday.

Ana wanted to give her brother a guitar for his birthday. She goes to the music store. It is very expensive. She looked at it and said I don't have enough money.

Ana thought of a way to earn money. She wants to wash cars. The sign says, "Car wash $5." She had two cars line up to get a car wash. She gets money to get a guitar. Her brother has the guitar. He said, "Thanks a lot. That's the one I wanted."

B   **1. Rewrite each sentence so it begins with part of the predicate.**

   2. Circle the subject and underline the whole predicate. Write N above any noun in the subject or P above the pronoun. Write V above the verb.

1. Their roof leaked during the rainstorm.
2. A young fox followed the bird without making a sound.
3. She walked outside after the big rainstorm.
4. The sun came out just before lunchtime.

INDEPENDENT WORK

C **Rewrite the underlined sentences so that the unclear word is clear.**

1. The clowns in the picture had stripes in their umbrella. <u>Don didn't like the way they looked.</u> He drew umbrellas that did not have stripes.
2. Martha got good grades from all of her teachers. <u>She was very happy with them.</u> They were the best grades she'd ever received.
3. Beth talked with Marge yesterday. <u>She was on her way to class.</u> Marge was sitting outside the office.

A   **Rewrite the passage so that all the sentences are correct.**

Ming was hungry when she got home

Ming was hungry when she got home from work. She sees nothing in the refrigerator. It is empty. She says Who ate all the food?

Ming solved her problem. She gets food from the grocery store. She bought steak, salad, and potatoes. She puts the food in her trunk and goes home. She put the food on the table. She said, "This is a great meal. I love steak and potatoes."

B   **Rewrite each sentence so it begins with part of the predicate. Remember the comma.**

1. Four dogs barked when the car started.
2. Our roof leaks when the rain blows from the north.
3. We went to a farm last week.

INDEPENDENT WORK

C WRITE INFORMATIVE TEXT

Source

The moose is the largest member of the deer family. The adult male moose is called a bull. Bulls are about six feet tall and weigh about 1,400 pounds. They have a growth of skin called a *bell* that hangs from their neck. The bull's antlers may measure six feet in width. The bull's coat is not a single color. The bull's body is blackish brown. The bull's face, legs, and belly are light brown.

The cow's coat is a single light-brown color. The calves are also light brown all over. Calves are born in the spring. The principal diet of the moose during the winter consists of leaves and twigs.

Statements   ### Outline Diagram

1. The bull moose is smaller than an adult deer.
2. The bull moose has something hanging from its neck.

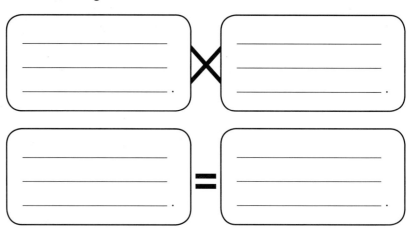

Check OD: Did you follow the **outline diagram** precisely?

Check S: Did you correctly **spell** all the words that are shown?

Check F: Did you write **parallel fact** sentences that support your conclusion?

▪ OD   ▪ S   ▪ F

D For each item, write a parallel response that starts with the word <u>no</u> and uses the word <u>also.</u>

1. Wise old men are the only people who are smart.
2. The only way Mary can get a good workout is by riding a bike fast.
3. The only way you can lose weight is by eating less.

END OF LESSON 24

A **Rewrite the passage so all the sentences are correct.**

The telephone rang while David was ironing a shirt.

David

Where is that smoke coming from? I hope David is all right.

His brother Avi

David's cellphone rang while he was ironing a shirt. He answered it. He talks to his friend a long time. The iron falls off the board. The clothes in the basket smoke.

Avi was hanging a picture on the wall upstairs. Avi sees it. Avi said Where is the smoke coming from? I hope David is all right. Avi goes downstairs to see what is up. David is still on the phone. Avi puts the fire out just in time.

INDEPENDENT WORK

B **For each item, write the simple past-tense verb.**

1. see   6. choose   10. eat

2. run   7. speak   11. get

3. sell   8. sit   12. take

4. go   9. fall   13. write

5. fly

END OF LESSON 25

A Fix all the problems in this passage.

Carlo talked to Becky while his sister Olga went to look at the bears.

Carlo talked to Becky while his little sister Olga went to look at the bears. Olga's doll is in the bear pit. Olga said, Help me. My doll fell into it. Becky got the zookeeper.

The zookeeper had an idea. She rode the elephant over to it. The elephant put her trunk in the pit. She said get it. She grabbed it with its trunk. She pulled it out and gave it to her. Olga gave her peanuts to eat.

INDEPENDENT WORK

B

1. Rewrite each sentence so it begins with part of the predicate.
2. For each rewritten sentence, circle the subject and underline the predicate. Then write <u>V</u> above the verb words, or <u>N</u> above any nouns in the subject.

1. Six boys walked to the fishing hole in the morning.
2. Our committee will meet with the mayor on Tuesday.
3. The house burned during the night.
4. The wind got stronger as the day got hotter.

C Rewrite the underlined sentence so the unclear word is clear.

1. Carl has stamps from each of the islands in the Caribbean. <u>They are small.</u> Bird Island is very small.
2. We loaned five books to the boys. <u>They were in great shape.</u> By next week, they will probably have bent pages.
3. My uncle loves to go out with little Billy. <u>He rides a tricycle.</u> Little Billy also has a tricycle.
4. That woman has a kitten in her coat pocket. <u>It is light colored.</u> The coat pocket is black.

A WRITE A STORY WITH DIALOGUE

Ming was hungry when she got home from work.

Who ate all the food?

Ming solved her problem.

This is a great meal. I love steak and potatoes.

| refrigerator | empty | nothing | meal | grocery store |
| bought | meat | steak | salad | potatoes | kitchen |

Check Q: Did you use quotes to tell the exact words somebody said?

Check M: Did you tell all the important things that must have happened?

Check RS: Did you begin each paragraph with the right sentence?

Check P: Is each sentence punctuated correctly?

☐ **Q**   ☐ **M**   ☐ **RS**   ☐ **P**

INDEGENDENT WORK

B Write about each statement. Use the appropriate outline diagram.

Statements

1. School lasts longer than three hours a day.
2. 25 plus 18 is less than 40.
3. Nickels are worth more than dimes.

Outline Diagram

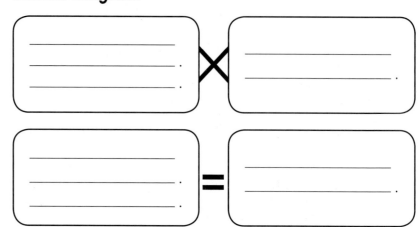

Check OD: Did you follow the **outline diagram** precisely?

Check S: Did you correctly **spell** all the words that are shown?

Check F: Did you write **parallel fact** sentences that support your conclusion?

☐ OD   ☐ S   ☐ F

C **1. Rewrite each sentence so it begins with part of the predicate.**

2. Circle the subject, underline the whole predicate, write <u>V</u> above the verbs, <u>N</u> above the noun in the subject, or <u>P</u> above the pronoun.

1. You may find the pathway home by going behind the building.
2. The girls finished their work at the end of the day.
3. The early birds look for worms early in the morning.

END OF LESSON 27

A **Write the sentence the first person is saying. Use the word <u>only</u>.**

1.

only _____ _____.

No, wasps and hornets are also flying insects that sting.

2.

only _____ _____.

No, trains are also land vehicles that transport heavy loads.

3.

only _____ _____.

No, crickets are also animals that make noise at night.

Ana wanted to give her brother a guitar for his birthday.

I don't have enough money.

Ana thought of a way to earn money.

Thanks a lot. That's the one I wanted.

earned	charged	sign	music store	price tag
enough	money	present	bought	birthday party

Check M: Did you tell all the important things that must have happened?

Check VT: Are all the verbs that tell what happened in the past tense?

Check Q: Did you use quote marks to show the exact words somebody said?

Check PC: Did you use the pronouns *he, she,* or *it* so they are clear?

Check P: Is each sentence punctuated correctly?

◼ **M**   ◼ **VT**   ◼ **Q**   ◼ **PC**   ◼ **P**

END OF LESSON 28

A Write the sentence the first person is saying. Use the word <u>only</u>.

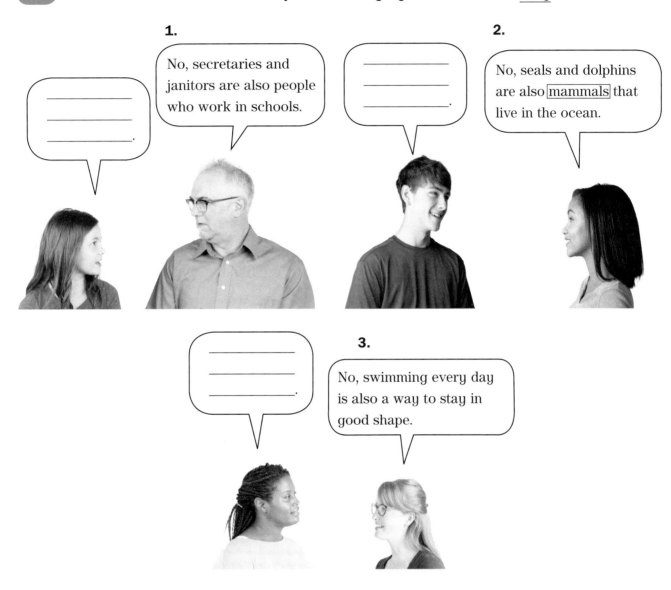

1.

No, secretaries and janitors are also people who work in schools.

2.

No, seals and dolphins are also mammals that live in the ocean.

3.

No, swimming every day is also a way to stay in good shape.

INDEPENDENT WORK

B Write the sentences with the adjectives in the right order.

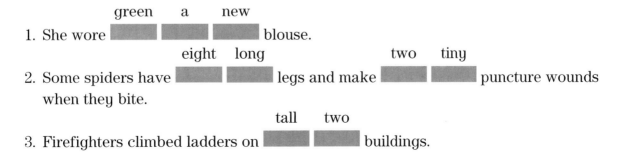

green   a   new

1. She wore ▭ ▭ ▭ blouse.

eight   long   two   tiny

2. Some spiders have ▭ ▭ legs and make ▭ ▭ puncture wounds when they bite.

tall   two

3. Firefighters climbed ladders on ▭ ▭ buildings.

Source Data

Softwood Species	Common Uses
Douglas Fir	piling, plywood, veneer, residential framing
Eastern White Pine	construction lumber, central layer of plywood paneling
Hemlock	containers, knotty paneling
Sugar pine	doors, frames, window blinds
Redwood	boards, joists, posts, outdoor furniture

Hardwood Species	Common Uses
Birch	cabinets, cupboards, plywood, veneer, doors
Black Cherry	furniture, caskets, fine veneer paneling
Mahogany	furniture, fine veneers, paneling
Red Oak	fence posts, truck floors
Teak	furniture, fine veneer paneling
Black Walnut	furniture, decorative paneling, cabinets

Statements

1. Pines are hardwoods.
2. Birch has many uses.
3. Black walnut is used for firewood.

Outline Diagram

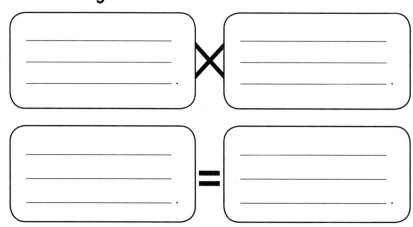

Check OD: Did you follow the **outline diagram** precisely?

Check S: Did you correctly **spell** all the words that are shown?

Check F: Did you write **parallel fact** sentences that support your conclusion?

☐ OD   ☐ S   ☐ F

END OF LESSON 29

A Write the sentence the first person is saying. Use the word **only**.

1.

_____
_____
_____.

No, the country of [Chile] borders both the Pacific Ocean and the Atlantic Ocean.

2.

_____
_____
_____.

No, blackberry bushes and thistles are also plants that have thorns.

3.

_____
_____
_____.

No, [Suriname] is also a South American country with an area of less than 65,000 square miles.

B   WRITE A STORY WITH DIALOGUE

David's cell phone rang while David was ironing a shirt.

David

Avi was hanging a picture on the wall upstairs.

Where is that smoke coming from? I hope David is all right.

His brother Avi

cell phone   next   room   smoke   fire extinguisher   sprayed   stairs
worried   clothes basket   through   doorway   downstairs   ironing board

Check M: Did you tell all the important things that must have happened?

Check VT: Are all the verbs that tell what happened in the simple past or past-progressive tense?

Check Q: Did you tell the exact words somebody said and punctuate the quotes correctly?

Check PC: Did you use the pronouns *he, she,* or *it* so they are clear?

Check W: Did you write at least two sentences that begin with a part that tells when?

☐ **M**   ☐ **VT**   ☐ **Q**   ☐ **PC**   ☐ **W**

END OF LESSON 30

A **Write a sentence that joins two sentences with a semicolon, however, and a comma.**

1. Donna agreed with him   his brother didn't agree.

2. Mr. Davis runs very fast   his wife can keep up with him.

B **WRITE A STORY WITH DIALOGUE**

> Carlo talked to Becky while his sister Olga went to look at the bears.

| bear | elephant | trunk | peanuts | rescued |
| fence | tumbled | leaned | lifted | |

Check M: Did you tell all the important things that must have happened?

Check VT: Are all the verbs that tell what happened in the simple past or past-progressive tense?

Check Q: Did you tell the exact words somebody said and punctuate the quotes correctly?

Check PC: Did you use the pronouns *he, she,* or *it* so they are clear?

Check W: Did you write at least two sentences that begin with a part that tells when?

■ **M**   ■ **VT**   ■ **Q**   ■ **PC**   ■ **W**

END OF LESSON 31

A Join the two sentences with <u>however</u>. Punctuate that part correctly.

She loved to sing.   Her voice was too loud.

B WRITE OPINION PIECE

Document M

Students usually go into fifth grade after fourth grade. Fifth graders are 15 years old. Young girls are shorter than boys of the same age.

Document M contains some inaccuracies.

Here's an outline diagram for writing about inaccuracies. This outline diagram includes an introduction box that tells about the number of inaccuracies, followed by X boxes that describe each inaccuracy.

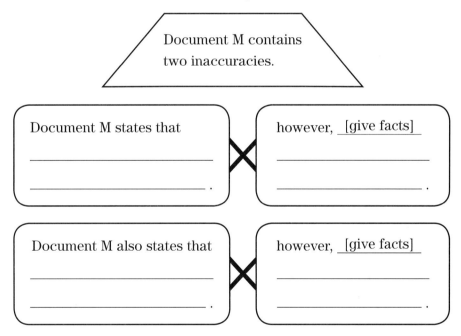

Here is the passage you could write about Document M using the outline diagram:

Document M contains two inaccuracies. Document M states that fifth graders are 15 years old; however, fifth graders are 10 or 11 years old. Document M also states that young girls are shorter than boys of the same age; however, young girls are taller than boys of the same age.

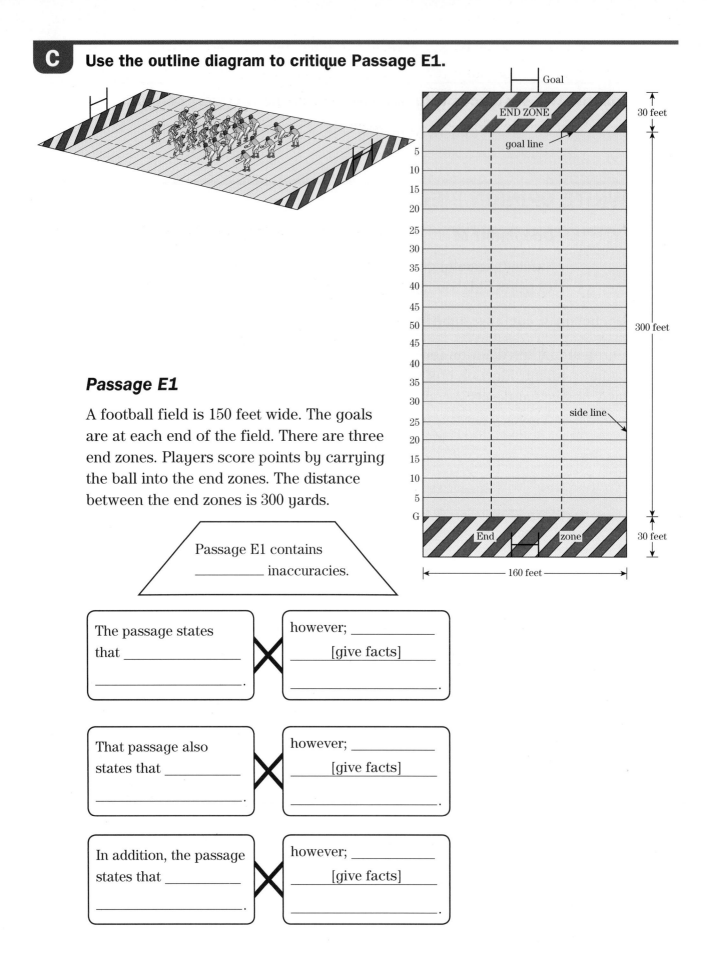

C Use the outline diagram to critique Passage E1.

Passage E1

A football field is 150 feet wide. The goals are at each end of the field. There are three end zones. Players score points by carrying the ball into the end zones. The distance between the end zones is 300 yards.

Passage E1 contains _____ inaccuracies.

The passage states that _____ _____ .

however; _____ _____ [give facts] _____ _____ .

That passage also states that _____ _____ .

however; _____ _____ [give facts] _____ _____ .

In addition, the passage states that _____ _____ .

however; _____ _____ [give facts] _____ _____ .

Check OD: Does the paragraph follow the **outline diagram** exactly?

Check P: Did you **punctuate** your sentences correctly?

Check F: Did your **fact** sentences give accurate parallel information?

Check S: Did you correctly **spell** all the words that are shown?

☐ OD   ☐ P   ☐ F   ☐ S

D **Correct the first statement in each item by writing a sentence that uses the words no and only.**

1. Girls and boys played at the picnic.
   Girls played at the picnic.

2. Girls played at the picnic and in the cabin.
   Girls played at the picnic.

3. Girls played and talked at the picnic.
   Girls played at the picnic.

END OF LESSON 32

A **Correct the first statement in each item by writing a sentence that uses the words no and only.**

1. The workers <u>rested and talked</u> during their break.
   The workers rested during their break.

2. The workers rested during their break.
   Some of the workers rested during their break.

3. The workers rested during their break and during their lunch hour.
   The workers rested during their break.

B **Use the outline diagram to critique Meg's passage.**

Source Map

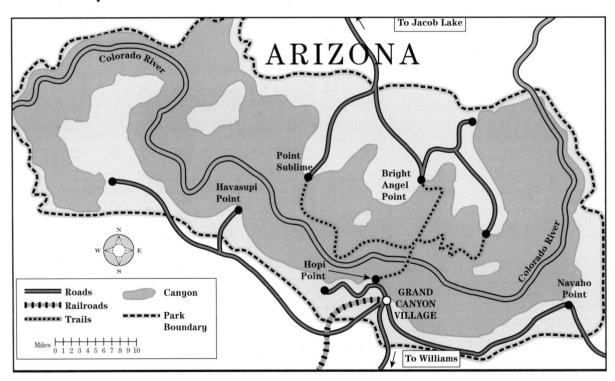

Grand Canyon National Park, Arizona

Meg's Passage

Grand Canyon National Park is about 55 miles wide. The Colorado River snakes through the park. There is a trail from Hopi Point to Bright Angel Point. Two railroad tracks are west of Grand Canyon Village. To the north of Grand Canyon National Park is Jacob Lake. The town of Williams is also north of Grand Canyon Village.

Outline Diagrams

Meg's passage contains _____ inaccuracies.

The passage states that _____ _____.

however; [give facts] _____ _____.

Check OD: Does the paragraph follow the **outline diagram** exactly?

Check P: Did you **punctuate** your sentences correctly?

Check F: Did your **fact** sentences give accurate parallel information?

Check S: Did you correctly **spell** all the words that are shown?

☐ OD   ☐ P   ☐ F   ☐ S

INDEPENDENT WORK

C Copy the sentences on your lined paper. Circle the subject, underline the predicate. Write V above the verb. Label the part of speech of all the words in the subject: N for noun, MN for main noun, A for adjective, Pr for preposition.

1. The children on the bus were safe.
2. The dogs in the park were happy.

D Write a parallel response to each sentence. Begin with the word no and use the word also.

1. Turtles are the only animals that lay eggs.
2. You can fish only in rivers.

END OF LESSON 33

34

A   **Tell why these statements are false by writing a correct sentence that has the words <u>no</u> and <u>only</u>.**

> ### *Sample Sentence*
>
> They painted the ceiling and the floor.
> (The ceiling is not painted.)
>
> No, they painted only the floor.

1. The doctor examined the children and their parents.
   (Parents did not receive examinations.)

2. The doctor examined and vaccinated the children.
   (No children received vaccinations.)

3. The doctor and nurse examined the children.
   (The nurse did not examine the children.)

INDEPENDENT WORK

B For each sentence, write two parallel sentences.

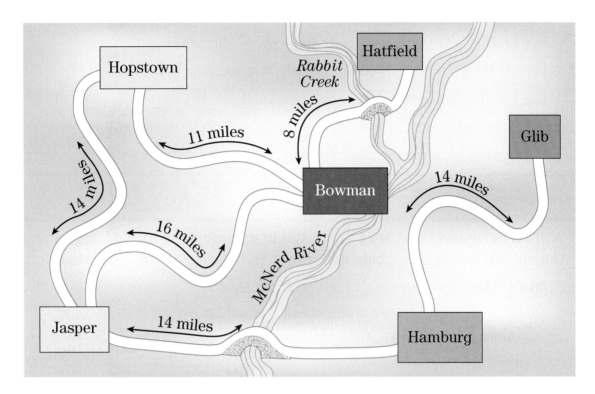

1. Hatfield borders the McNerd River.
2. Hopstown is more than 10 miles from Bowman.
3. Jasper is 14 miles from Hamburg.

C
1. **Rewrite each sentence so it begins with part of the predicate.**
2. **For each rewritten sentence, circle the subject and underline the whole predicate. Write N above the noun or P above the pronoun in the subject. Write V above every verb word.**

1. Fifteen students went to lunch after finishing the math assignment.
2. One student will receive a special award next week.
3. The magician pulled a rabbit from his hat without pausing.
4. We walked home after the movie.

END OF LESSON 34

A **Write responses that use the words no and only. Think about the fact in parentheses to put only in the right place.**

1. Her brother and her sister repaired the chair.
   (Her sister did not work on the chair.)

2. Her brother repaired the chair and painted it.
   (The chair is not painted.)

3. Her brother repaired the chair and the couch.
   (The couch still needs repair.)

B **Write a paragraph that tells about the inaccuracies in Ethan's passage. Use the outline diagram to guide you. Refer to the source for accurate information.**

Ethan's Passage

Before telephones were invented, Morse code was used to send messages over long distances. The person sending the message would press a key to make a signal. Morse code has dots and dashes.

To send a dot, the sender holds the key down for a very short period. To send a dash, the sender holds the key down for a longer period.

To send the word man, the sender would send the combination of dots and dashes for the letters m, a, n:

m is ▬▬
a is •▬
n is ▬•

The next group of dots and dashes is supposed to spell the word eggs, but there is a mistake.

e is •
g is ▬▬•
g is ▬▬•
s is ••

Source

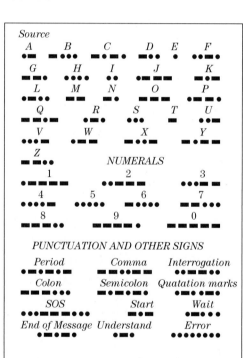

A sender sends the word **not** to indicate the end of the message.

n is ▬•
o is ▬▬▬
t is ▬

Outline Diagrams

Ethan's passage contains _____ inaccuracies.

The passage states that _____ _____ .

however; _____ _____ _____ .

Check OD: Does the paragraph follow the outline diagram exactly?

Check P: Did you punctuate your sentences correctly?

Check F: Did your **fact** sentences give accurate parallel information?

Check S: Did you correctly **spell** all the words that are shown?

☐ OD   ☐ P   ☐ F   ☐ S

INDEPENDENT WORK

C Write responses that use the words <u>no</u> and <u>only</u>. Think about the fact in parentheses to put <u>only</u> in the right place.

1. All hounds drank from the pond.
   (Some of the hounds did not drink.)

2. The hounds drank from the pond and swam in the pond.
   (No hounds swam.)

3. They fixed the car and cleaned up the mess.
   (They didn't clean up anything.)

D Rewrite the sentence on your lined paper so the verbs are in the past tense, either past-progressive or simple past tense. Underline the verbs.

1. Mike and Jamal are sitting under a tree when they heard a loud noise.
2. He is telling the story again because Jena was not there the first time.
3. Molly was choosing the best pies for the fair because she knows good pies.
4. I am writing a story while Mia sang a song.

END OF LESSON 35

A **The statements in parentheses are true. Correct the first statement in each item by writing a parallel sentence that starts with <u>no</u> and uses the word <u>only</u>.**

1. The wolves howled and ate at night.
   (The wolves did not eat.)

2. All the wolves howled at night.
   (Some did not howl.)

3. The wolves howled at night and in the afternoon.
   (The wolves did not howl in the afternoon.)

B **Use the facts to tell what is wrong with the statements. Follow the X-box diagram.**

1. Justin, Gina, and Julie went to the store.
   Fact: Julie stayed home.

2. Yen's brother swept and washed the garage floor.
   Fact: The garage floor was not washed.

3. Three types of ducks and two types of geese flew down from Canada.
   Fact: One type of goose was from Canada.

Statement _____ indicates that _____ _____ ;	however, that statement is inaccurate. [Tell why.] _____ .

Check OD: Did you follow the **outline diagram** precisely?

Check F: Did you write **parallel fact** sentences that use the word **only?**

Check S: Did you correctly **spell** all the words that are shown?

☐ **OD**   ☐ **F**   ☐ **S**

C LINK IDEAS

- You've learned when you indicate what somebody says, you use the word **that**.
- Here's something you would write:

  Statement 1 indicates that the moose is a large animal.

- You wouldn't write:

  Statement 1 indicates the moose is a large animal.

- You use the word **that** with all ideas that are expressed as a sentence.
- Here's a sentence:

  Lulu knows her mother.

  You don't need the word **that** because **her mother** is not a sentence.

  Lulu knows the alphabet.

  You don't need the word **that** because **the alphabet** is not a sentence.

  Lulu knows that winter is near.

  You need the word **that** because **winter is near** is a sentence.

D Write statements that tell what Lulu knows.

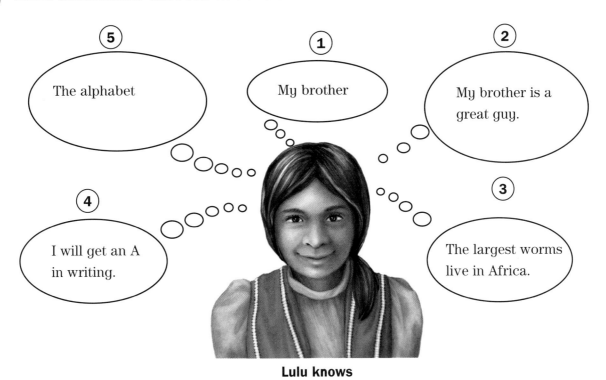

5 The alphabet

1 My brother

2 My brother is a great guy.

4 I will get an A in writing.

3 The largest worms live in Africa.

Lulu knows

END OF LESSON 36

A Use the facts to tell what is wrong with statements 1 and 2. Follow the X-box diagram.

Source: **An Advertisement for Clipper Boats**

If you buy a brand-new Clipper boat right now, you'll save four ways.

First, you'll save $10 on the windshield.
You'll save more than $500 on the engine.
You'll save $200 on the custom seats.
And you'll save $10 on the owner's manual.

Remember, when you buy a Clipper, you get clipped.

Facts

These things are reduced in price:
windshield .... reduced $10
custom seats .... reduced $200
owner's manual ...... reduced $10

Outline Diagram

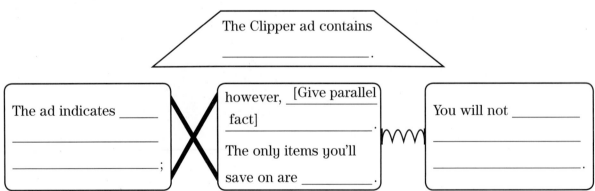

The Clipper ad contains _____.

The ad indicates _____ _____ _____;

however, [Give parallel fact] _____.
The only items you'll save on are _____.

You will not _____ _____ _____.

Check OD: Did you follow the **outline diagram** precisely?

Check F: Did you write **parallel fact** sentences that use the word **only?**

Check S: Did you correctly **spell** all the words that are shown?

▇ OD   ▇ F   ▇ S

Write statements that tell the ideas that Hondo underlines.

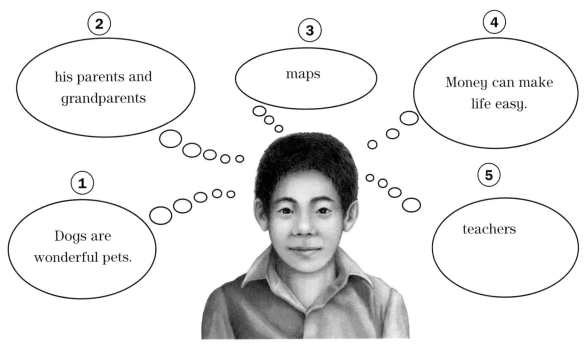

Hondo believes

C   **The second sentence in each item gives correct information. Start with the word No, and write sentences that have the word only.**

1. The hounds chased the fox and caught the fox.
   (They did not catch the fox.)

2. All of the hounds chased the fox.
   (Some did no chasing.)

3. The hounds and the hunters chased the fox.
   (The hunters did not chase the fox.)

4. The hounds chased the fox and the rabbit.
   (There was no rabbit.)

END OF LESSON 37

A Emma believes all the things that are listed. For each item, write a sentence that tells what Emma believes. Emma believes. . .

1. Three is more than two
2. Everything she reads on the internet
3. Her father
4. People should eat healthy food

B On your lined paper, write the main noun and the correct verb for each item.

               is are
1. The basket of clothes [   ] dirty.

           was were
2. The lot of cars [   ] for sale.

           was were
3. The bottles of juice [   ] leaking.

           is are
4. The seats on the bus [   ] redone with seatbelts.

           is are
5. The house of cards [   ] famous.

INDEPENDENT WORK

C
1. Rewrite each sentence so it begins with part of the predicate.
2. For each rewritten sentence, circle the subject and underline the whole predicate. Write **N** above the noun in the subject. Write **V** above every verb word.

1. Our car stopped between the towns of Glick and Glump.
2. The show began just before the thunder started booming.
3. Dan hummed his song during the entire dinner show.

D The second sentence in each item gives correct information. Start with the word No, and write sentences that have the word <u>only</u>.

1. The hounds drank from the pond.
   (Some of the hounds did not drink.)

2. The hounds drank from the pond and swam in the pond.
   (No hounds swam.)

3. They fixed the car and cleaned up the mess.
   (They didn't clean up anything.)

END OF LESSON 38

INDEPENDENT WORK

A Write a paragraph that tells about the inaccuracies in the passage. Use the outline diagram to guide you. Refer to the source map for accurate information.

Source Map

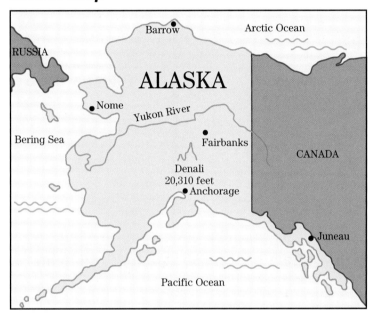

Passage

Alaska is the largest state in the United States. Alaska borders Canada and Norway. The highest mountain in North America is in Alaska. That mountain is Denali. It is 30,200 feet high. The town that is farthest north in Alaska is Barrow. The city that is farthest south is Juneau.

Outline Diagram

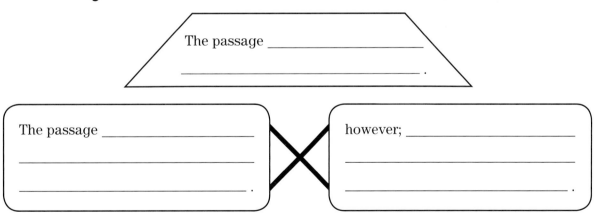

Check OD: Did you follow the **outline diagram** precisely?

Check F: Did you write **parallel fact** sentences that support your conclusion?

Check S: Did you correctly **spell** all the words that are shown?

    ■ OD   ■ F   ■ S

B The second sentence in each item gives correct information. Start with the word No, and write sentences that have the word <u>only</u>.

1. All the students finished their work.
   (Some did not finish.)

2. The students and their teachers went on a trip.
   (The teachers did not go on the trip.)

3. The students finished their work and went on a trip.
   (No one went on a trip.)

C The items tell the things that Margaret states. For each item, write a sentence that begins with the words <u>Margaret states</u>.

1. Her name.
2. She should eat nutritious foods.
3. The order of topics.
4. The argument is contradictory.

D On your lined paper, write the correct past-tense verb for each item.

Present	Past
1. go	
2. catch	
3. lose	
4. buy	
5. write	
6. come	
7. feel	
8. hear	
9. tell	
10. find	

END OF LESSON 39

A GRAMMAR CONVENTIONS

Some sentences are unclear because words that tell where or when are in the wrong place.

- Here's a sentence that has a clear meaning:

  In 1975, they studied the history of birds.

- Here's a sentence that is not clear:

  They studied the history of birds in 1975.

- That sentence has two meanings. The two pictures show the two meanings.

A

B

Each sentence has more than one meaning. Write the silly meaning for the second picture.

1. They discussed their future in the kitchen.

2. Mark went to a meeting on fishing with four friends.

3. We watched the rockets take off from our couch.

END OF LESSON 40

A **Each sentence has more than one meaning. Write the silly meaning for the second picture.**

1. He bought a tool for cleaning his furnace at the store.

2. They watched thousands of geese flying from their yard.

3. Olga says she knows how birds communicate on the phone.

Write each sentence in the present-progressive tense.

1. Five ducks swim around the pond.
2. The oldest boy guards the others.
3. Clouds make shade in the valley.
4. Her phone rings frequently.

C WRITE A STORY WITH DIALOGUE

Start a new paragraph each time a different person talks.

Check M: Did you tell all the important things that must have happened?

Check VT: Are all the verbs that tell what happened in the simple past or past-progressive tense?

Check CP: Did you punctuate each sentence correctly with capitals, periods, commas, and quote marks?

Check P: Did you make a new paragraph each time a different person talks?

Check S: Did you correctly spell all the words that are shown?

☐ **M**   ☐ **VT**   ☐ **CP**   ☐ **P**   ☐ **S**

INDEPENDENT WORK

D
Rewrite the underlined sentences so that the unclear word is clear.

1. The clowns in the picture had stripes on their umbrellas. <u>Don didn't like the way they looked.</u> He drew umbrellas that did not have stripes.

2. Ebba got good grades from all of her teachers. <u>She was very happy with them.</u> They were the best grades she'd ever received.

3. Beth talked with Sophie yesterday. <u>She was on her way to class.</u> Sophie was sitting outside the office.

E
On lined paper, write the main noun and the correct verb for each sentence.

1. A bunch of onions ▒▒▒▒ still on the counter.   **was   were**

2. A chest of drawers ▒▒▒▒ in every bedroom of the house.   **is   are**

3. A creature with six legs ▒▒▒▒ crawling over my hand.   **is   are**

4. Four children with their father ▒▒▒▒ in the car.   **was   were**

5. The oldest chairs in the office ▒▒▒▒ thrown away.   **was   were**

END OF LESSON 41

A **For each item, write the more general meaning in the first picture and the more specific, silly meaning in the second picture.**

1. They learned about arguing in school.

2. Mr. Briggs told how he worked on 18 bridges yesterday.

3. They discussed the new freeway in the library.

asked   answered   muttered

Check M: Did you tell all the important things that must have happened?

Check VT: Are all the verbs that tell what happened in the simple past or past-progressive tense?

Check CP: Did you punctuate each sentence correctly with capitals, periods, commas, and quote marks?

Check P: Did you make a new paragraph each time a different person talks?

Check S: Did you correctly spell all the words that are shown?

▪ **M**   ▪ **VT**   ▪ **CP**   ▪ **P**   ▪ **S**

C CONVEY IDEAS PRECISELY

When you write clearly, you don't use the words **this** or **that** without also using a noun that names **this** or **that**.

Here's writing that is not clear: **Tim jumped 12 feet. That made him the champ.** The second sentence says, *That* made him the champ. The sentence doesn't name what made him the champ.

Here's the item written clearly: **Tim jumped 12 feet. That jump made him the champ.**

Here's another unclear item: **The sales decreased in March. That worried the owner of the company.** The second sentence doesn't name what worried the owner.

Here's the item written clearly: **The sales decreased in March. That decrease worried the owner of the company.**

END OF LESSON 42

43

A Punctuate each sentence.

> "We have to go home now," he said.

1. are you feeling well he asked
2. did you stay out late last night his mom asked
3. I got home early he said
4. we ran four miles Ann yelled
5. did you find the shirt you were looking for she asked
6. that dog is very friendly Tom said to himself

B Fix these unclear sentences by moving the confusing part to the beginning of the sentence. Put a comma after the part you move.

1. Mr. Briggs told how he worked on 18 bridges yesterday.
2. We watched thousands of geese take off from our yard.
3. Mary learned how birds communicate during the last month.
4. He bought a tool for cleaning his furnace at the store.

INDEPENDENT WORK

C Edit this passage. Write sentences that are not run-ons and that do not have inappropriate words.

    They've ants in they're kitchen there going to hire Bug Busters to make sure their kitchen don't have no bugs. Its going to be a big job.

Follow the outline diagram to write about the problems in Tim's account. Make sure that your sentences are clear.

Accurate Source

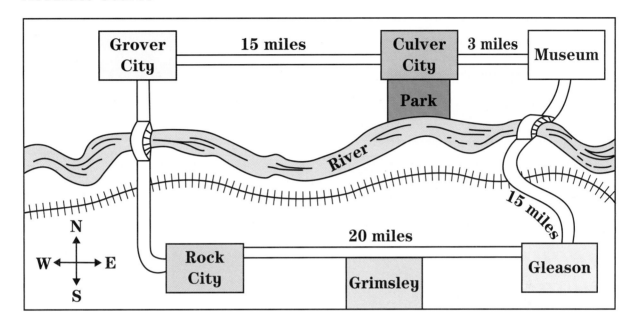

Tim's Account

We left Grover City in the morning and drove about 8 miles to Culver City.

We had breakfast in a park just outside Culver City. The park was right on the river.

After breakfast, we drove south 3 miles to the museum. We looked at a lot of old boats.

Then we went south again about 15 miles to the town of Gleason. My cousin lives there, and we visited with her for a while. We had lunch with her.

Then we drove about 20 miles west to the town of Grimsley. We bought some stuff there. Then we drove back to Grover City.

Check OD: Did you follow the outline diagram precisely?

Check F: Did you write parallel fact sentences that tell accurate information?

Check S: Did you correctly spell all the words that are shown?

■ OD   ■ F   ■ S

Outline Diagram

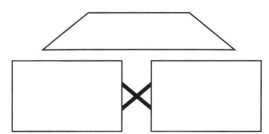

E **Write each verb in the simple past tense.**

Present	Past
1. go	
2. catch	
3. lose	
4. buy	
5. write	
6. come	
7. feel	
8. hear	
9. tell	
10. find	

END OF LESSON 43

A **Write a silly meaning. Rewrite the original sentence so it does not have a silly meaning.**

1. They discussed the farm animals they saw in school.

   We saw _____ .
   _____ .

2. We read how Columbus sailed to America last year.

   I sailed to _____ .
   _____ .

3. I found a book about repairing bikes in our basement.

   This book _____ .
   _____ .

B REASONING

You've worked with pairs of sentences that are the same except for one part. That part makes one of the sentences more general than the other sentence.

For each pair of sentences, you can make a **deduction.**

Here are the rules for making deductions:

✓ Write the more general sentence first.

✓ Skip a line. Write **Therefore, comma,** and the more specific sentence.

✓ Underline the part of each sentence that makes it more general or more specific.

✓ Make up a middle sentence by combining the underlined parts.

✓ Start the middle sentence with the more specific part.

1. All humans need air.

   All grandmothers need air.

2. Kayla King studies.

   All students study.

C Rewrite the passage. Punctuate sentences that tell the exact words somebody said.

	Tom loved to tell jokes. One day, he walked up to his brother and said can I ask you a question
	You sure can his brother said
	Why did the chicken cross the road Tom asked
	I don't know his brother said.
	The chicken crossed the road to get to the other side Tom said his brother laughed and laughed. He loved that joke.

END OF LESSON 44

A WRITE A STORY WITH DIALOGUE

> Susie and Alex were getting ready to cook dinner when they heard a loud noise inside the cave.

stretched   stood   away   scared   roared   furry

Check M: Did you tell all the important things that must have happened?

Check P: Did you make a new paragraph each time a different person talks?

Check UW: Did you avoid writing unclear words?

Check W: Did you begin at least one sentence with a part that tells when?

Check CP: Did you punctuate each sentence correctly with capitals, periods, commas, and quote marks?

Check S: Did you correctly spell all the words that are shown?

☐ **M**   ☐ **P**   ☐ **UW**   ☐ **W**   ☐ **CP**   ☐ **S**

Write a complete deduction for each item.

1. All vertebrates have a liver. All lizards have a liver.

2. All plants grow. All living things grow.

C **Write a silly meaning. Rewrite the original sentence so it does not have a silly meaning.**

1. We listened to the professor's account about capturing elephants in our classroom.

   I captured ▭
   ▭

2. We saw a movie about a terrible war last night.

   A terrible war took place ▭
   ▭

3. We asked him how much his sister grew yesterday.

   How much did your ▭
   ▭

INDEPENDENT WORK

D **Rewrite this passage. Write sentences that are not run-ons and that do not have inappropriate words.**

The best way to keep you're heart in good shape is to run that'll make your heart beat faster it'll beat more than 90 times per minute.

E **On your lined paper, write the letter of the sentence that is more specific.**

1. a. Martha works every afternoon.
   b. Martha will work on Wednesday afternoon.

2. a. My Uncle Pete makes furniture.
   b. All my relatives make furniture.

3. a. Those workers built all the houses on Donner Street.
   b. Those workers built the house at 114 Donner Street.

4. a. All rivers contain fresh water.
   b. The Red River contains fresh water.

F **On lined paper, write the main noun and the correct verb for each sentence.**

1. Several squirts of mustard ▭ still on the counter.   **was   were**

2. A house of mirrors ▭ a fun place to visit.   **is   are**

3. A box of crayons ▭ spilled all over the floor.   **is   are**

4. The best cookies in town ▭ found at Smith's Grocery.   **was   were**

5. The most famous actors in Hollywood ▭ appearing at the theater.
   was   were

A Write a complete deduction for each item.

1. You can trust Nathan. You can trust all your close friends.
2. Liquids flow. Water flows.
3. You should try to do all jobs well. You should try to do schoolwork well.

B Answer the question for each sentence.

Item 1: What was in the garage?
   a. The bats in the garage heard a noise.
   b. The bats heard a noise in the garage.

Item 2: What came from Mexico?
   a. An old man delivered a package from Mexico.
   b. An old man from Mexico delivered a package.

Item 3: What was in New York?
   a. A company in New York sent a price list to its customers.
   b. A company sent a price list to its customers in New York.

WRITE A STORY WITH DIALOGUE

> Bill and James were disappointed with the robot they had just assembled.

wrecked   fishbowl   scared   TV   flower   pot

Check M: Did you tell all the important things that must have happened?

Check P: Did you make a new paragraph each time a different person talks?

Check UW: Did you avoid writing unclear words?

Check W: Did you begin at least one sentence with a part that tells when?

Check CP: Did you punctuate each sentence correctly with capitals, periods, commas, and quote marks?

Check S: Did you correctly spell all the words that are shown?

☐ **M**   ☐ **P**   ☐ **UW**   ☐ **W**   ☐ **CP**   ☐ **S**

INDEPENDENT WORK

D Write a general meaning and more specific meaning for the sentence. Then make the original sentence clear.

They discussed why birds migrate on Monday.

I'm not sure why
_____
_____.

General meaning: ▬▬▬▬▬▬▬▬

Specific silly meaning: ▬▬▬▬▬▬▬

Clear original sentence: ▬▬▬▬▬▬▬

E Rewrite each sentence by moving part of the predicate to the beginning of the sentence. Punctuate sentences correctly.

1. The soup cooked on the stove while it rained outside.
2. We visited my uncle the day before yesterday.
3. We played softball against the Spartan team last Friday.
4. We do better in school when we go to bed early.

END OF LESSON 46

A INFORMATIVE TEXT

Notes:

- volcanoes—erupt, explode
- lava mountains—Hawaiian Islands
- Mt. St. Helens—1980

Check I: Did you explain the idea of each note?

Check SP: Did you write every sentence so it has a subject and a predicate?

Check CP: Did you punctuate every sentence correctly with capitals, periods, commas, and quote marks?

Check S: Did you correctly spell all the words that are shown?

☐ I　　☐ SP　　☐ CP　　☐ S

B Write a complete deduction for each item.

1. You should be polite to grandmothers. You should be polite to older people.
2. All monkeys have lungs. All mammals have lungs.
3. All birds lay eggs. Penguins lay eggs.

C Answer the question for each sentence.

Item 1: What was near the river?
 a. People near the river saw three planes.
 b. People saw three planes near the river.

Item 2: What was under the maple tree?
 a. The squirrels watched a crow under the maple tree.
 b. The squirrels under the maple tree watched a crow.

INDEPENDENT WORK

D **On your lined paper, rewrite this passage. Punctuate the sentences correctly and fix inappropriate words.**

They're dog was all black. At night he was hard to see. Their cat was the same color. she made a loud purring noise when you petted her. Very good at catching mice. Our cat is not black he don't make a loud purring noise.

A WRITE A STORY WITH DIALOGUE

replied   asked   explained   answered   muttered

Check M: Did you tell all the important things that must have happened?

Check P: Did you make a new paragraph each time a different person talks?

Check UW: Did you avoid writing unclear words?

Check IE: Did you give your story an interesting ending?

Check CP: Did you punctuate each sentence correctly with capitals, periods, commas, and quote marks?

Check S: Did you correctly spell all the words that are shown?

■ **M**   ■ **P**   ■ **UW**   ■ **IE**   ■ **CP**   ■ **S**

B **Each pair of sentences has a part that is the same. Write what that part refers to.**

Item 1: What occurred in the morning?
   a. The hike had difficult moments in the morning.
   b. The hike in the morning had difficult moments.

Item 2: What occurred in April?
   a. The vacation in April had a long rainy period.
   b. The vacation had a long rainy period in April.

C **REVISE AND EDIT**

[1]James picked flowers. [2]He put them inside his house. [3]A large bunch of bright red flowers was on the kitchen table. [4]Five vases of flowers were in the dining room. [5]A rose with many yellow petals were in the living room. [6]The windows of the garage were decorated with blue flowers. [7]A large bunch of yellow daisies were in the hall.

A WRITE INFORMATIVE TEXT

Referring to a **source** can make your writing more convincing.

Your source can be a graph, a table, a map, or a passage that gives **accurate information.**

The source circle behind an introductory box in the outline diagram tells you to name your source.

If you take your facts from a source labeled Graph E4, you'd start your introductory sentence with these words: **According to Graph E4.**

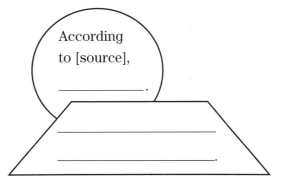

WRITE INFORMATIVE TEXT

Tony's Account

I earn $2,440 each month. I save $300 every month. I pay about the same amount for food as I do for rent. My auto expenses are $350 each month. My entertainment expenses are $200 each month. My only remaining expense is taxes.

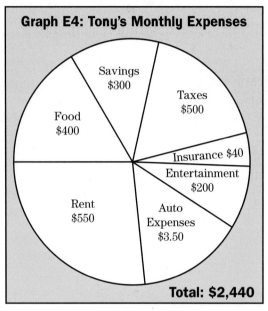

Graph E4: Tony's Monthly Expenses

Savings $300

Taxes $500

Food $400

Insurance $40

Entertainment $200

Rent $550

Auto Expenses $3.50

Total: $2,440

Outline Diagram

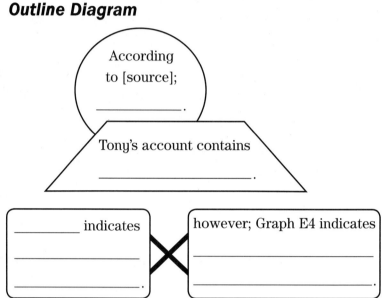

According to [source]; _____.

Tony's account contains _____.

_____ indicates _____ _____.

however; Graph E4 indicates _____ _____.

Check IF: Did you correctly identify inaccurate facts?

Check SF: Did you provide facts from the source that support your conclusion?

Check OD: Did you follow the outline diagram precisely?

Check S: Did you correctly spell all the words that are shown?

■ IF   ■ SF   ■ OD   ■ S

END OF LESSON 50

A **For each sentence, write what the words <u>between the rivers</u> refer to.**

1. The city between the rivers had a large business district.
2. The city had a large business district between the rivers.

B **For each sentence, write the letter of each picture the sentence <u>could</u> refer to.**

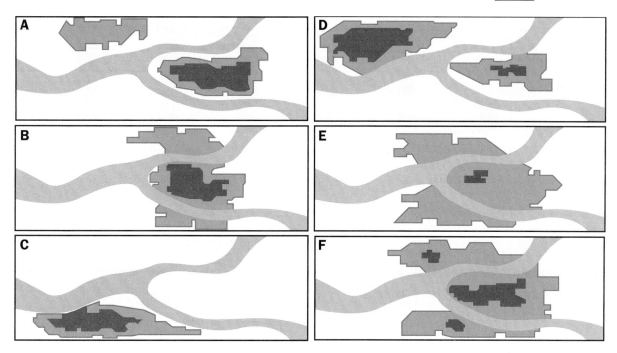

1. The city between the rivers had a large business district.
2. The city had a large business district between the rivers.

C **For each item, write these sentences and the missing sentence to make a complete deduction.**

1. Ducks have feathers.
   Birds have feathers.

2. Jobs are hard to find.
   A teaching job is hard to find.

3. Insects have six legs.
   Flies have six legs.

4. All mammals are warm-blooded.
   Whales are mammals.

D **Here is Bryan's account and a graph that shows accurate facts. Check Bryan's account for inaccuracies. Follow the outline diagram to write a paragraph about the inaccuracies.**

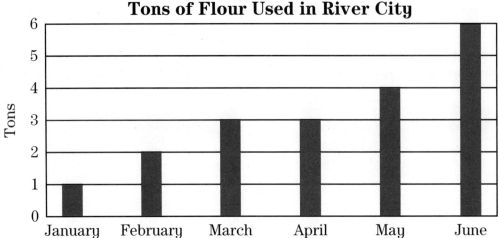

Source: Graph E3
Tons of Flour Used in River City

Bryan's Account

   River City used between one ton and six tons of flour each month from January through June. In March, River City used three tons of flour. In April, River City used four tons of flour. In June, River City used three tons more flour than it used in May.

Outline Diagram

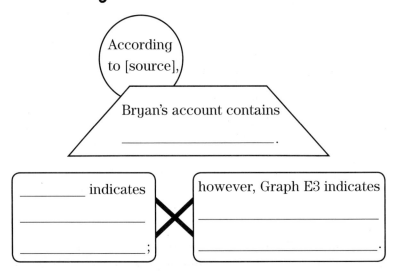

According to [source],

Bryan's account contains
_____.

_____ indicates
_____
_____;

however, Graph E3 indicates
_____
_____.

Check IC: Did you correctly identify inaccurate claims?

Check SF: Did you provide facts from an accurate source to support your conclusion?

Check OD: Did you follow the outline diagram precisely?

Check S: Did you correctly spell all the words that are shown?

◼ **IC**   ◼ **SF**   ◼ **OD**   ◼ **S**

END OF LESSON 51

A **For each sentence, write what the words <u>next to the farm</u> refer to.**

1. The forest next to the farm had a grove of maples.
2. The forest had a grove of maples next to the farm.

B **For each sentence, write the letter of each picture the sentence <u>could</u> refer to.**

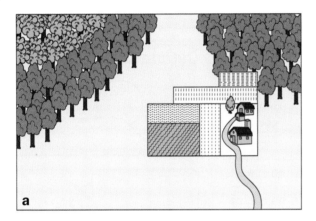

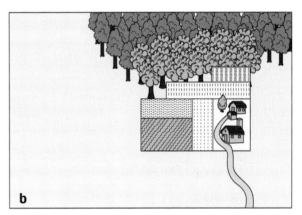

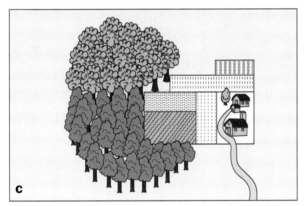

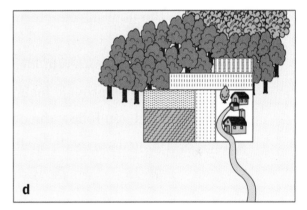

1. The forest next to the farm had a grove of maples.
2. The forest had a grove of maples next to the farm.

C Follow the outline diagram. Write a summary sentence, and then write about each inaccuracy in the ad.

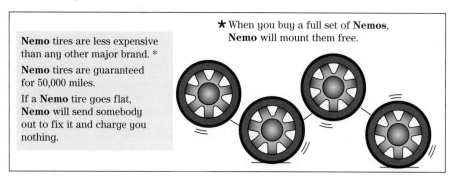

Nemo tires are less expensive than any other major brand. *

Nemo tires are guaranteed for 50,000 miles.

If a **Nemo** tire goes flat, **Nemo** will send somebody out to fix it and charge you nothing.

★ When you buy a full set of **Nemos**, **Nemo** will mount them free.

Source: Table E1: Major Brand Tires

Tires	Cost per tire	Guaranteed for	Cost of mounting	Cost for roadside service
Nemo	$45.50	50,000 miles	no cost	$25
Brand A	$42.50	50,000 miles	$5 each tire	no charge
Brand X	$51.17	70,000 miles	no cost	no charge

Outline Diagram

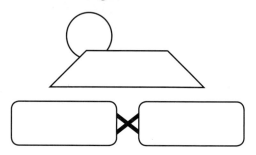

Check IS: Did your introductory statement name the source and state the number of inaccuracies?

Check IC: Did you correctly identify inaccurate claims?

Check SF: Did you provide facts from an accurate source to support your conclusion?

Check OD: Did you follow the outline diagram precisely?

Check S: Did you correctly spell all the words that are shown?

▥ **IS**   ▥ **IC**   ▥ **SF**   ▥ **OD**   ▥ **S**

INDEPENDENT WORK

D Use the sentences that are shown to write deductions. Put the more specific sentence in the conclusion. Write the missing middle sentence.

1. Martha works every afternoon.
   Martha will work on Wednesday afternoon.

2. My Uncle Pete makes furniture.
   All my relatives make furniture.

3. Those workers built all the houses on Donner Street.
   The workers built the house at 114 Donner Street.

4. All rivers contain fresh water.
   The Red River contains fresh water.

E **Write the general meaning sentence, the specific silly meaning sentence, and the original sentence so it is clear.**

They discussed why birds migrate on Monday.

1. General meaning
2. Specific silly meaning
3. Clear original sentence

A TAKE NOTES AND CLASSIFY INFORMATION

Vocabulary

redwood	half	California	height
building	forest	inches	giant

1. **main thing**

   details

Copy this outline on your lined paper:

1. **tallest trees**

2.

3.

Check N: Did you explain each note clearly and accurately?

Check SP: Did you write each sentence with a subject and a predicate?

Check CP: Did you begin each sentence with a capital and end with a period?

Check S: Did you correctly spell all the words that are given?

Make a box for each check.

☐ N   ☐ SP   ☐ CP   ☐ S

B For each sentence, write what is near the river.

1. People saw three planes near the river.
2. People near the river saw three planes.

Write the letter of every picture each sentence could describe.

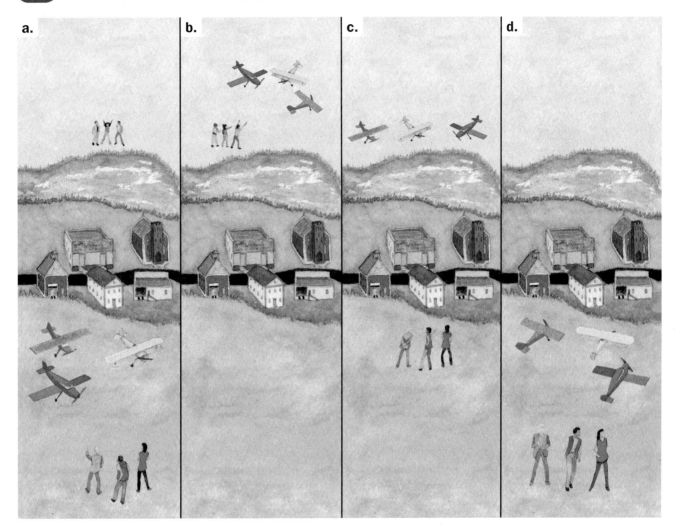

a. b. c. d.

1. People saw three planes near the river.
2. People near the river saw three planes.

For each sentence, write <u>who was sitting in a chair.</u>

1. The man who was sitting in a chair talked to a woman.
2. The man talked to a woman who was sitting in a chair.

Write the letter of every picture each sentence could describe.

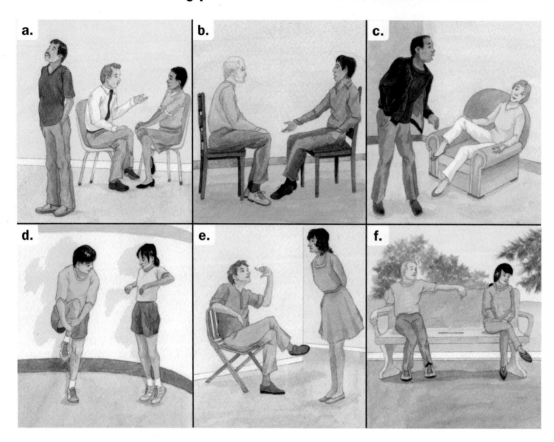

a.   b.   c.

d.   e.   f.

1. The man who was sitting in a chair talked to a woman.
2. The man talked to a woman who was sitting in a chair.

INDEPENDENT WORK

F   **Use the sentences that are shown to write deductions. Put the more specific sentence in the conclusion. Write the missing middle sentence.**

1. The workers painted the office.
   The workers painted every room in the school.

2. All legal papers are legal documents.
   His license is a legal document.

G   **Rewrite each sentence so it is clear.**

1. Ginger told me about her sister's marriage on the telephone.
2. My brother described how tigers hunt after school.
3. Mr. Briggs indicated that he would help us fix the garage in a long letter.
4. We discussed ways we could help unfortunate children on our back porch.
5. We watched the planes fly over the river from our front porch.

END OF LESSON 53

A TRANSFORM STATEMENTS TO QUESTIONS

Here's a rule: Parts of speech are the same for a statement and a parallel question that uses the same words. The subject and predicate are also the same.

Here's a **statement** with a two-word verb:

The girls **could walk** to school.

Here's a **parallel question** that uses all the words in the statement:

Could the girls **walk** to school?

The question has the same verb words as the original statement.

B For each statement, write a parallel question that uses the same words. Circle the subject and underline both parts of the predicate. Write N for the noun and A for the adjective in the subject. Write P if the subject is a pronoun. Write V for each verb word in the predicate.

1. That boy was running in the street.
2. My little sister can jump rope.
3. Mary should buy new shoes.
4. You would do the same thing next time.
5. She has bought expensive hats before.

C Rewrite the sentence so it tells about each picture. Add the words <u>in the yard</u>.

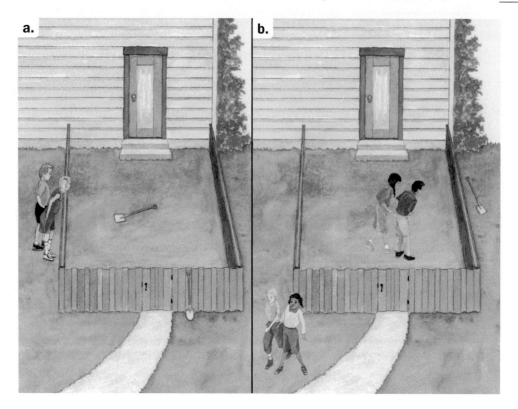

The children saw a shovel.

INDEPENDENT WORK

D Write the second sentence in each item so the meaning is clear.

1. Jan arranged the flowers very carefully. She was proud of that.
2. She increased her strength with lots of weight-lifting exercises. That made her happy.
3. The doctor explained the problem. We took notes on that.
4. The crew extended the parking lot 40 feet. That made it possible to park buses in the lot.

E Use the sentences that are shown to write deductions. Put the more specific sentence in the conclusion. Write the missing middle sentence.

1. My uncle drives a Bumpo.
   All my relatives drive Bumpos.

2. All dangerous chemicals were removed from the factory.
   XXD4 was removed from the factory.

Follow the outline diagram. Write a summary sentence, and then write about each inaccuracy in the ad.

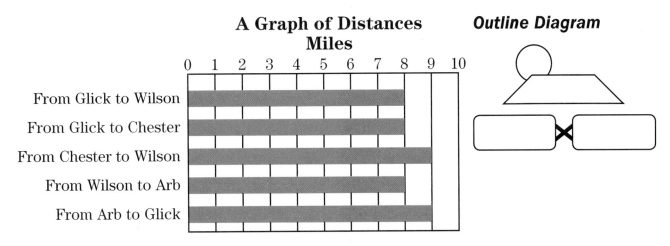

A Graph of Distances
Miles

Outline Diagram

0 1 2 3 4 5 6 7 8 9 10

From Glick to Wilson
From Glick to Chester
From Chester to Wilson
From Wilson to Arb
From Arb to Glick

Accurate Source: **Map E3**

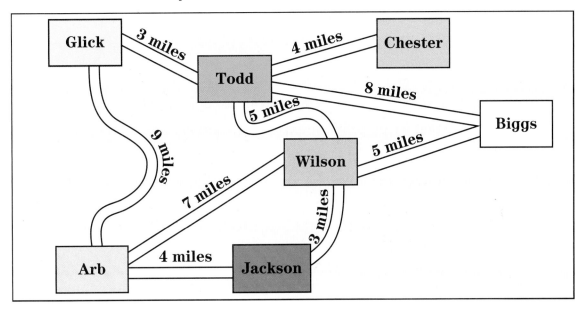

Check IS: Did your introductory statement name the source and state the number of inaccuracies?

Check IC: Did you correctly identify inaccurate claims?

Check SF: Did you provide facts from an accurate source to support your conclusions?

Check OD: Did you follow the outline diagram precisely?

Check S: Did you correctly spell all the words that are shown?

☐ IS   ☐ IC   ☐ SF   ☐ OD   ☐ S

A TAKE NOTES AND CLASSIFY INFORMATION

Vocabulary

raised	animals	different	vegetable	popcorn
America	wheat	field	Native Americans	rice

1. **main thing**

   details

Copy this outline on your lined paper:

1. grain

2.

3.

Check N: Did you explain each note clearly and accurately?

Check SP: Did you write each sentence with a subject and a predicate?

Check CP: Did you begin each sentence with a capital and end with a period?

Check S: Did you correctly spell all the words in the vocabulary box?

    ◼ **N**   ◼ **SP**   ◼ **CP**   ◼ **S**

B Make each statement into a parallel question that uses the same words.
Circle the subject. Underline the predicate.
Write N above every noun in the subject.
Write A above every adjective in the subject.
Write V above every verb in the predicate.

1. Your neighbors could help us.
2. Those students do know how to cook.
3. Our teacher was watching that movie.

C Rewrite the sentence so it tells about each picture. Add the words <u>on the window sill</u>.

The cat looked at the mouse

INDEPENDENT WORK

D Use the sentences that are shown to write deductions. Put the more specific sentence in the conclusion. Write the missing middle sentence.

1. All the documents that Herbert made were inaccurate.
   The map of Rono was inaccurate.

2. Timmy has a picture of a square.
   Timmy has a picture of every kind of rectangle.

END OF LESSON 55

A TAKE NOTES AND CLASSIFY INFORMATION

> **Vocabulary**
>
> human   size   flea   inches   fields   record

> 1. **main thing**
>
>   **details**

Copy this outline on your lined paper:

1. **high jump**

2.

Check N: Did you explain each note clearly and accurately?

Check SP: Did you write each sentence with a subject and a predicate?

Check CP: Did you begin each sentence with a capital and end with a period?

Check S: Did you correctly spell all the words in the vocabulary box?

☐ N   ☐ SP   ☐ CP   ☐ S

B Rewrite the sentence so it tells about each picture. Add the words with a long tail.

a.   b.

The cat chased the kite.

C Make parallel statements that use all the words in the question.
Circle the subject. Underline the predicate.
Write **N** above every noun in the subject.
Write **A** above every adjective in the subject.
Write **V** above every verb in the predicate.

1. Were the little bugs crawling all over your yard?
2. Is that tire losing air?
3. Was her car getting dirty?
4. Should mean dogs stay inside?

INDEPENDENT WORK

D Write a complete deduction for each pair of sentences. Show the more specific sentence as the conclusion of the deduction.

1. She collects shirts.
   She collects objects made of cloth.

2. Iron floats in mercury.
   Iron floats in liquids that are more dense than iron.

END OF LESSON 56

A TAKE NOTES AND CLASSIFY INFORMATION

Vocabulary

load   human   flea   distances   mammal

1. main thing

   details

Copy this outline on your lined paper:

1. types of fleas

2.

3.

Check N: Did you explain each note clearly and accurately?

Check SP: Did you write each sentence with a subject and a predicate?

Check CP: Did you begin each sentence with a capital and end with a period?

Check S: Did you correctly spell all the words in the vocabulary box?

   ☐ **N**   ☐ **SP**   ☐ **CP**   ☐ **S**

B Make parallel statements that use all the words in the question.
Circle the subject. Underline the predicate.
Write N above every noun in the subject.
Write A above every adjective in the subject.
Write V above every verb in the predicate.

1. Could a sentence have a short subject?
2. Does the old car run well?
3. Will his last test cover 20 lessons?
4. Is their favorite entertainer coming to town?

INDEPENDENT WORK

C Rewrite each sentence so it is clear.

1. We asked if her tree was still growing fast yesterday.
2. They told us about their trip around the world in less than twenty minutes.
3. We watched a shooting star streak across the sky from the kitchen window.

END OF LESSON 57

A WRITE A STORY WITH DIALOGUE

first	then	next	later	before	after
during	finally	replied	asked	explained	

Check D: Was the story detailed enough to answer most questions a reader would have?

Check PS: Was the problem acceptably solved in the end?

Check NS: Did you make a new paragraph for each new speaker?

Check Q: Did you properly punctuate the sentences with quotes?

Check V: Did you use most of the vocabulary words?

☐ D   ☐ PS   ☐ NS   ☐ Q   ☐ V

B Write parallel questions that use all the words in the statement.
Circle the subject. Underline the predicate.
Write **N** above the noun in the subject.
Write **A** above every adjective in the subject.
Write **V** above both verbs.

1. An adjective could be in a question.
2. Her sentences are getting better.
3. The other workers were loading trucks.
4. His brother is watching her.
5. A music class will give a performance.

INDEPENDENT WORK

C Rewrite the sentence so it tells about each picture. Add the words <u>near the bush</u>.

a. b.

The bear watched the bunny.

A EXPLAIN EVIDENCE

- Some claims are **inaccurate.** They're false.

- Other claims are **misleading.** They're true, but they're right on the edge of being false. They give a false impression, but they are not really false.

- Here are two pillows:

Dandy

Floppo

$19 \frac{1}{2}$ ounces

19 ounces

- This claim is inaccurate:

    Dandy pillows weigh a lot more than Floppo pillows.

- This claim is inaccurate:

    Dandy pillows are lighter than Floppo pillows.

- This claim is **true,** but **misleading:**

    Floppo pillows are lighter than Dandy pillows.

- This claim is **true** and **not misleading:**

    Floppo pillows are slightly lighter than Dandy pillows.

- This claim is true, not misleading, and **very specific:**

    Floppo pillows are $\frac{1}{2}$ an ounce lighter than Dandy pillows.

- Remember, claims that are true but that refer to very small differences may be misleading.

For each item, write whether a claim is true or false. Then write the number of any claim that is misleading.

Bumpo
2,700 pounds

Sinko
2,702 pounds

Statements:

1. Bumpo weighs two pounds less than Sinko.
2. Bumpo and Sinko weigh the same amount.
3. Bumpo weighs less than Sinko.
4. Sinko weighs a lot more than Bumpo.
5. Sinko weighs two pounds less than Bumpo.

C **Rewrite each question as a statement. Circle the subject. Underline the predicate. Label all the words in the subject, N for noun, A for adjective, and P for pronoun. Write V above the verb words in the predicate.**

1. Are they going to the beach?
2. Could your sister buy an extra pen?
3. May I go home?
4. Will the ants move those leaves?

D WRITE A STORY WITH DIALOGUE

I tried to hit the basket.

Ben

first	then	next	later	before	after
during	finally	replied	asked	explained	

Check D: Was the story detailed enough to answer most questions a reader would have?

Check PS: Was the problem acceptably solved?

Check NS: Did you make a new paragraph for each new speaker?

Check Q: Did you properly punctuate the sentences with quotes?

Check V: Did you use some of the vocabulary words?

☐ D   ☐ PS   ☐ NS   ☐ Q   ☐ V

END OF LESSON 59

A WRITE A STORY WITH DIALOGUE

Rover, behave yourself.

Mr. Briggs

Janice

first   then   next   later   before   after
during   finally   replied   asked   explained   answered

Check D: Was the story detailed enough to answer most questions a reader would have?

Check PS: Was the problem acceptably solved in the end?

Check NS: Did you make a new paragraph for each new speaker?

Check Q: Did you properly punctuate the sentences with quotes?

Check V: Did you use most of the vocabulary words?

■ D   ■ PS   ■ NS   ■ Q   ■ V

B Change each question to a statement. Circle the subject. Underline the predicate. Label all the words in the subject, N for noun, A for adjective, and P for pronoun. Write V about the verb words in the predicate.

1. Can all those clowns fit in that tiny car?
2. Will he know how to find our house?
3. Are the younger children doing well in school?
4. Have the birds eaten all the food?

A **Write about an experience that frightened you.**

Outline Diagram

> Paragraph 1: [Use words from the directions] occurred [tell when].
> [Tell where]. [Summarize what happened to frighten you.]
>
> Paragraph 2: [Tell details of what happened—what you did.]
> [Tell how you felt at the end.]

Check D: Did you give enough detail to answer most questions a reader would have?

Check OD: Did you follow the outline diagram precisely?

Check VT: Did you use verbs that are in the past tense or past-progressive tense?

Check Q: Did you include quotations?

Check P: Did you correctly punctuate all the sentences?

☐ **D**　　　☐ **OD**　　　☐ **VT**　　　☐ **Q**　　　☐ **P**

INDEPENDENT WORK

B **Write each statement as a question. Punctuate the sentence correctly. Circle the subject. Underline the predicate.**
Write N above every noun.
Write A above every adjective.
Write P above every pronoun.
Write V above every verb.

1. All the puppies have had lunch.
2. The clouds do indicate rain.
3. The sled dogs can pull the sled.

END OF LESSON 61

A WRITE OPINION PIECE

Spuddo ad

A **Spuddo** bike weighs less than a Yusha.
A **Spuddo** bike costs less than a Yusha.

Standard equipment includes:
an 11-speed drive train,
a bike computer,
and disc brakes.

Source: **Bike Facts**

- Weight of Spuddo: 15 pounds
- Cost of Spuddo: $375.99
- Weight of Yusha: 20 pounds
- Cost of Yusha: $376.00
- Standard equipment: 11-speed drive train, disc brakes
- Additional equipment available: headlight, rear fender, bike computer

Outline Diagram

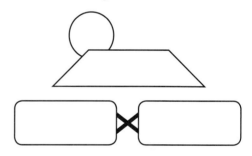

Check IS: Did your introductory sentence name the source and identify the type of problems?

Check IC: Did you correctly identify inaccurate claims?

Check MC: Did you write clearly about any misleading claim?

Check OD: Did you follow the outline diagram precisely?

Check S: Did you correctly spell all the words that are shown?

☐ IS   ☐ IC   ☐ MC   ☐ OD   ☐ S

B Rewrite each sentence so it has a noun and an adjective in place of the pronoun.

> *Sample Item*   **They** loved **it.**
> **Four girls** loved **the party.**

1. They looked at it.
2. She kept smelling it.
3. He walked around it.

END OF LESSON 63

A **Write about an experience that embarrassed you.**

Outline Diagram

> Paragraph 1:   [Use words from the directions] occurred [tell when].
> [Tell where]. [Tell what happened.]
>
> Paragraph 2+:   [Give enough information for the reader to know details of
> what happened.]
>
> Last paragraph: [Tell how you felt at the end.]

Check D: Did you give enough detail to answer most questions a reader would have?

Check OD: Did you follow the outline diagram precisely?

Check VT: Did you use verbs that are in the past tense or past-progressive tense?

Check Q: Did you include quotations?

Check P: Did you correctly punctuate all the sentences?

▪ **D**   ▪ **OD**   ▪ **VT**   ▪ **Q**   ▪ **P**

Sample Passage

An experience that embarrassed me occurred last year. I was selected to get my picture taken with Clyde Johnson on the school playground. He is the famous basketball star who gave a lot of money for our playground equipment. I was so excited to get to meet him.

I was feeling special because I was one of only ten people selected for the picture with Clyde. We were supposed to wear our school uniforms. My mother brought me a clean shirt and sweater to put on just before the picture, so I would look neat and tidy. The sweater had our school name on it. I put the clothes on and went outside to the playground. There I saw Clyde with some other kids. He was chatting and laughing with the kids, when I ran up to him to give him a high five. I said my name was Alvin. Clyde said, "Hi, Alvin. What is the name of your school?"

I thought he should know where he was, so his question puzzled me at first. I looked down to where the school name was supposed to be on my sweater. It wasn't there. I had my sweater on inside out! I laughed in embarrassment and turned my sweater around.

When they finally took the picture, Clyde had his arm around my shoulders. He wanted me to get over my embarrassment and feel comfortable with him. Clyde Johnson is a great guy.

Write each sentence. Then circle the subject and underline the predicate.
Write P above every pronoun.
Write N above every noun.
Write A above every adjective.
Write Pr above every preposition.
Write V above every verb.

1. Big Bill pulled a wagon of them.
2. Four girls wore the same kind of bathing suit.
3. They played with it.
4. Margo tagged him.
5. Tiffany's kite was caught in a tree.
6. Henry carried them.
7. The men loved the game of horseshoes.

C
Rewrite each sentence so it has a noun and two adjectives in place of each pronoun.

1. Big Bill pulled a wagon of them.
2. Jane and her sister played with it.
3. Margo and Terry pushed it.
4. Henry carried them.

INDEPENDENT WORK

D **Rewrite each statement as a question. Punctuate correctly.**
For each sentence you rewrote, circle the subject, underline the predicate.
Write N above every noun.
Write A above every adjective.
Write P above every pronoun.
Write Pr above every preposition.
Write V above every verb.

1. The workers could take hours on that job.
2. Those dark clouds are moving in our direction.
3. She would have that fixture.
4. The Jones family did stop in the town of Redding.

END OF LESSON 64

A WRITE OPINION PIECE

Posho ad

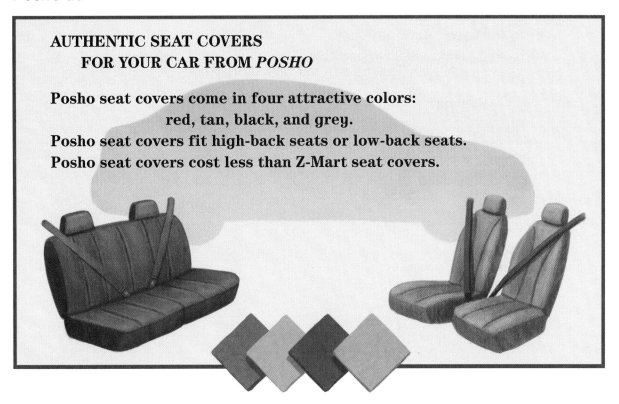

AUTHENTIC SEAT COVERS FOR YOUR CAR FROM *POSHO*

Posho seat covers come in four attractive colors: red, tan, black, and grey.
Posho seat covers fit high-back seats or low-back seats.
Posho seat covers cost less than Z-Mart seat covers.

Source: Seat Cover Facts

- Colors: tan, grey, black
- Fits: low-back seats only
- Cost of seat covers: $29.99 each
- Cost of Z-Mart seat covers: $59.99 a pair

Outline Diagram

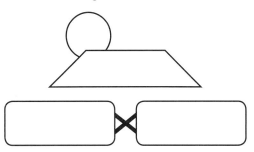

Check IS: Did your introductory sentence name the source and identify the type of problems?

Check IC: Did you correctly identify inaccurate claims?

Check MC: Did you write clearly about any misleading claim?

Check OD: Did you follow the outline diagram precisely?

Check S: Did you correctly spell all the words that are shown?

 IS   IC   MC   OD   S

List the topics from most general to most specific.

> **Topics arranged from more general to more specific:**
>
> Fish
>
> Ocean Fish
>
> Ocean Fish That Spawn in Coastal Streams
>
> Salmon
>
> King Salmon

1. bones of the face
   molars
   teeth
   12-year molars
   bones

2. basketball
   games
   ball games
   team ball games
   activities

A REPLACE NOUNS WITH PRONOUNS

A **pronoun** is more general than the **noun** it replaces.

For the noun **boys,** the pronoun is **they.**

For the noun **car,** the pronoun is **it.**

For the noun **James,** the pronoun is **he.**

Elephants eat grass.

B Change each sentence so it has no nouns, only pronouns.

Pronouns for nouns that are subjects	Pronouns for nouns that are not subjects
I	me
we	us
you	you
he	him
she	her
it	it
they	them

1. George is watching birds.

2. Fred and Carlos build houses.

3. Sand flew at Mary.

4. Dad chased Kevin.

Follow the outline diagram to write about the misleading impression in Rod's account.

Rod Vernon's account

I can't believe that my neighbors, the Jacksons, did the mean things they did. My dog, Herman, is usually on a leash, but once in a while, he goes out by himself. When this happens, he may run into the Jacksons' yard.

Last week, Herman dug a hole in the Jacksons' yard. And you would not believe the fuss they made about it. They called the police. They tried to get me arrested. They wanted to take Herman away and lock him up. All that fuss for digging one hole in their backyard! I can't believe that the Jacksons could be so unreasonable.

Outline Diagram

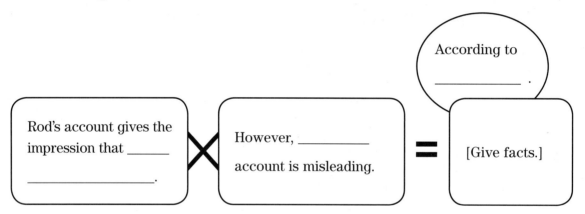

According to _____ .

Rod's account gives the impression that _____ _____ .

However, _____ account is misleading.

[Give facts.]

Check OD: Did you include all the words given in the outline diagram?

Check M: Did you clearly describe the misleading impression?

Check AS: Did you write **according to** and name your source?

Check F: Did you provide facts that show why the impression is misleading?

Check S: Did you correctly spell all the words that are shown?

◼ **OD**   ◼ **M**   ◼ **AS**   ◼ **F**   ◼ **S**

D List the topics from most general to most specific.

1. Single Mothers

   People

   Women

   Women Who Are Mothers

   Working Mothers Who Are Single

2. Working People

   Mail Carriers in Alabama

   People

   Mail Carriers in Montgomery, Alabama

   Mail Carriers

E Answer each question with a word that uses one of the prefixes or suffixes you've learned.

1. What word means **not kind?**

2. What word means **to view before?**

3. What word means **full of respect?**

4. What word means **not usual?**

5. What word means **one who prints?**

6. What word means **without harm?**

7. What word means **being tough?**

8. What word means **the opposite of allow?**

INDEPENDENT WORK

F Rewrite this passage. If the sentence is unclear, fix it to make it clear. If a sentence has more than one "and," you'll need to make more sentences.

Our teacher told us about dinosaurs on a field trip. We visited a place that had dinosaur bones with explanations. They were all around and we talked about them and discussed the past. That was interesting. Our teacher said that some dinosaurs ate plants on the bus.

END OF LESSON 66

A **List the topics from most general to most specific.**

1. Things Made of Glass
   Objects
   Transparent Objects
   Windows
   Stained Glass Windows

2. Little League Baseball Players
   Athletes
   Little League Baseball Team in Reno
   Baseball Players

B **Follow the outline diagram to write about the misleading impression in Matt's account.**

Matt's account

I can't believe how silly some people are. The people in our neighborhood are always complaining about walking across the railroad tracks. There's always a train going by, and they have to wait a long time before they can get across. There's a shopping mall on the other side of the tracks, and people could easily walk there, but walking across those railroad tracks is a serious problem.

So I offered a serious solution. Why not build a footbridge over the tracks? Everybody could get together, donate their time and some material, and we could build a footbridge.

What did the neighbors say when I told them about my solution? They said, "You're nuts."

Well, I happen to think that my solution makes a lot of sense.

Outline Diagram

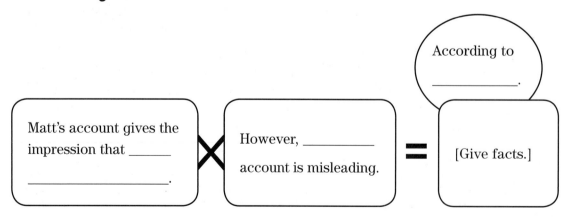

Check OD: Did you include all the words given in the outline diagram?

Check M: Did you clearly describe the misleading impression?

Check AS: Did you write **according to** and name your source?

Check F: Did you provide facts that show why the impression is misleading?

Check S: Did you correctly spell all the words that are shown?

☐ **OD**　　☐ **M**　　☐ **AS**　　☐ **F**　　☐ **S**

C **Rewrite each sentence so it has no nouns, only pronouns.**

1. Izzy and Jamie looked at old photo albums.
2. Pete watched them run around a barn.
3. My sisters were walking behind a yellow pony cart.
4. Benito watched James crawl under the old boards.
5. Rita hated those boring arguments.

D DETERMINE THE MEANING OF UNKNOWN WORDS

New root words:

　　photo　　　auto　　　tele　　　hydro　　　homo

1. photograph
2. automatic
3. telephone
4. hydroelectricity
5. homogenized

1.

Non homogenized　Homogenized

2.

E **Answer all the questions.**

| photo | auto | tele | hydro | homo |

1. Which prefix means **far?**
2. Which prefix means **the same?**
3. Which prefix means **self?**
4. Which prefix means **water?**
5. Which prefix means **light?**

INDEPENDENT WORK

F **Rewrite each question as a statement.**

1. Can David run as fast as Julie?
2. Were you considering all the possibilities?
3. Should young kittens go far from their mother?

END OF LESSON 67

A **Write about a regrettable event.**

Outline Diagram

Paragraph 1:   [Use words from the directions] occurred [tell when].
[Tell where]. [Tell what happened.]

Paragraph 2+:   [Give enough information for the reader to know details of
what happened.]

Last paragraph: [Tell how you felt at the end.]

Check D: Did you give enough detail to answer most questions a reader would have?

Check OD: Did you follow the outline diagram?

Check VT: Did you use verbs that are in the past tense or past-progressive tense?

Check Q: Did you include quotations?

Check P: Did you correctly punctuate all the sentences?

■ D   ■ OD   ■ VT   ■ Q   ■ P

INDEPENDENT WORK

B **Rewrite each sentence so pronouns replace all the nouns and their adjectives.**

1. Both boys loved the national park.
2. George was watching his favorite movie.
3. My three best friends celebrated my birthday.
4. Their largest pumpkin filled her wagon.

END OF LESSON 68

A **Follow the outline diagram to write about Lisa's account.**

Lisa's account

Sometimes parents are unreasonable. My parents told me that I could have a party on my sixteenth birthday. I told them that I didn't even want a present if I could have a party. They said, "Okay."

But then, just a couple of days before my birthday, they got all upset about the party, and they told me that they would never let me have another one.

Outline Diagram

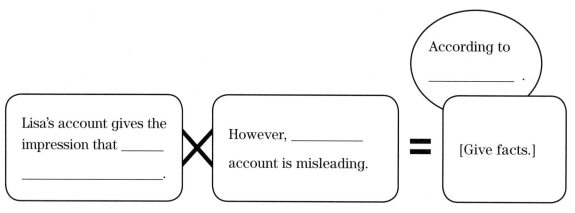

Lisa's account gives the impression that _____ _____.

However, _____ account is misleading.

According to _____ .

[Give facts.]

Check OD: Did you include all the words given in the outline diagram?

Check M: Did you clearly describe the misleading impression?

Check AS: Did you write **according to** and name your source?

Check F: Did you provide facts that show why the impression was misleading?

Check S: Did you correctly spell all the words that are shown?

▢ OD   ▢ M   ▢ AS   ▢ F   ▢ S

B **Write the word part each item describes.**

auto	phon	homo	photo
hydro	tele	graph	

1. What word part means **water?**
2. What word part means **far?**
3. What word part means **sound?**
4. What word part means **light?**
5. What word part means **self?**
6. What word part means the **same?**
7. What word part means to write or **draw?**

INDEPENDENT WORK

C **Change each sentence so pronouns replace all the nouns and their adjectives.**

1. The boys chased the dogs around the park.
2. Our car drove through the hills.
3. Their team will play three games.

END OF LESSON 69

A   Follow the outline diagram to tell about the problem with the argument.

Here's what Phil said:

I know three men who have long hair.
All of them are lazy.
Therefore, all men with long hair are lazy.

Passage

Phil concludes that all men with long hair are lazy; however, his conclusion is more general than the evidence. Evidence about three men with long hair cannot lead to a proper conclusion about all men with long hair.

Outline Diagram

Phil concludes that _____ _____ _____ .	however, his conclusion is more general than the evidence. Evidence about [a specific category] cannot lead to a proper conclusion about [a general category].

Here's what Rita said:

1. This pizza came from Tony's.
   The pizza is terrible.
   Therefore, all food from Tony's is terrible.

Outline Diagram

Rita concludes that _____ _____ _____ .	however, her conclusion is more general than the evidence. Evidence about [a specific category] cannot lead to a proper conclusion about [a general category].

Here's what Mark said:

2. Tom is from Calhoun County.
   Tom is tall.
   Therefore, all men from Calhoun County are tall.

Outline Diagram

Mark concludes that _____ _____ _____ .

however, his conclusion is more general than the evidence. Evidence about [a specific category] cannot lead to a proper conclusion about [a general category].

B DETERMINE THE MEANING OF UNKNOWN WORDS

1. **Transamerica** Airlines started operating in the late 1930s.
2. It took four years to complete the **transaction.**
3. They will **transplant** four thousand little cherry trees.
4. They remodeled the house and completely **transformed** it.

C Write the correct word for each sentence.

| transaction | transposed | hydrograph |
| transform | homogenous | transport |

1. The sale of the four buildings involved a ▓▓▓▓▓ that lasted over a year.

2. The ▓▓▓▓▓ showed the changing water levels of the Granby River.

3. They remodeled their apartment to completely ▓▓▓▓▓ it.

4. There were four kinds of rocks in the group, so it was not a ▓▓▓▓▓ sample.

5: It took five boxcars to ▓▓▓▓▓ all the furniture.

INDEPENDENT WORK

D Rewrite this passage. In some sentences, you may need to move part of the predicate.

There was a beautiful bird in our backyard we didn't know what kind it was it's head was bright red it's eyes were orange. We told my mother about the bird in the kitchen. She indicated that some woodpeckers were building they're nest nearby. She said that their getting ready to lay eggs.

END OF LESSON 70

A Follow the outline diagram to tell about the problem with the argument.

Harry's argument: Jane is rich.

Jane is from Billtown.

Therefore, everybody from Billtown must be rich.

Outline Diagram

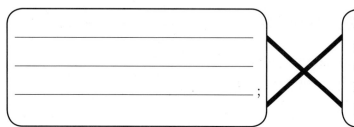

however, the conclusion is more general than the evidence. Evidence about [a specific category] cannot lead to a proper conclusion about [a general category].

A Follow the outline diagram to write about the problem with the argument.

Here's what Irene said:

I know that everybody in our class voted for Kim to be the new school president. Therefore, everybody in the whole school must have voted for Kim.

Outline Diagram

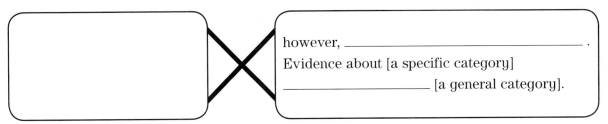

however, ———————————————— .
Evidence about [a specific category]
—————————————— [a general category].

A **Rewrite each sentence so it uses forms of the words <u>inundate</u> or <u>arduous</u> wherever possible. Use the words correctly so your sentence makes sense.**

1. Thousands of letters flooded the radio station.
2. They began a very difficult journey.
3. It took days of hard work to clean up the flooded town.

B **Write about the problem with Cecilia's argument.**

Here's what Cecilia said:

I was in the gym at Dunn School. The gym was very noisy. Therefore, Dunn School must be a terribly noisy place.

END OF LESSON 73

A TAKE NOTES AND WRITE ORGANIZED PASSAGE

Vocabulary:

Denali   North Pole   boundary   Canada
North American   sea level   peak

Alaska borders the northwest corner of Canada. The north boundary of Alaska is only 1,300 miles from the North Pole.

Alaska is the largest state in the United States. Alaska has the highest mountain in North America. That mountain is Denali. Its peak is four miles above sea level.

Notes:

Alaska

1. location

2. physical features

Check N: Did you explain each note clearly and accurately?

Check O: Did you use your own sentences?

Check SP: Did you write every sentence so it has a subject and a predicate?

Check CP: Did you begin each sentence with a capital and end with a period?

Check S: Did you correctly spell all the words in the notes and in the word list?

Make a box for each check.

☐ **N**   ☐ **O**   ☐ **SP**   ☐ **CP**   ☐ **S**

END OF LESSON 74

A TAKE NOTES AND WRITE ORGANIZED PASSAGE

Vocabulary:

treasure	buried	island
pounds	inches	cube

Buried Treasure

The treasure is buried on the first island north of the mainland. It is buried five yards west of the tallest oak tree.

The treasure is a block of gold. The block is a twelve-inch cube. It weighs over 500 pounds.

Check N: Did you explain each note clearly and accurately?

Check O: Did you use your own sentences?

Check SP: Did each sentence have a subject and a predicate?

Check CP: Did you begin each sentence with a capital and end with a period?

Check S: Did you correctly spell all the words in the notes and the word list?

Make a box for each check.

☐ N   ☐ O   ☐ SP   ☐ CP   ☐ S

B Rewrite these sentences so they use fancy words you've learned.

Word list:

inundate	expunge	arduous

1. They tried to get rid of an ink spot.
2. This work is far too difficult for children.
3. Sid got rid of all the ants that were in his house.
4. Water from the broken dam flooded River City.

END OF LESSON 75

A Write a passage answering the question about "Work and Goals." Use the Outline Diagram to write your passage.

Question

Why do you think Al would have performed better if he had followed the coach's training program?

Outline Diagram

Al would have performed better if he had followed the coach's training program. [Compare Diego's training and performance with Al's training and performance.]

Check OD: Did you follow the outline diagram exactly?

Check 4S: Did write at least 4 sentences?

Check P: Did you correctly punctuate your sentences?

Check VT: Did you always use the past tense to tell what happened?

☐ OD　　　☐ 4S　　　☐ P　　　☐ VT

B Rewrite each sentence so it uses one of the words from the word list.

Word list	inundate	arduous	expunge

1. I could not remove those terrible images from my mind.
2. The pilgrims began a difficult journey.

INDEPENDENT WORK

C These sentences have errors. Rewrite each sentence so it is correct.

1. Mark say that he is sick.
2. The boys pulled a lot of weeds after it rained, so they were very wet and tired.
3. He don't think of other people sometimes.
4. We waited for an hour, but he don't show up.

END OF LESSON 76

A TAKE NOTES AND WRITE ORGANIZED PASSAGE

Vocabulary:

sequoia   Sierra   general   Nevada
Sherman   Fresno   weigh   National   California

General Sherman

The biggest living thing on Earth is a sequoia tree named General Sherman. The tree is 275 feet tall and 102 feet around. The bark is 24 inches thick. The tree weighs over 2,000 tons and is 3,000 years old.

General Sherman is located in the Sequoia National Park in California. The park is in central California. It is in the Sierra Nevada mountain range. The park is about 60 miles east of Fresno, California.

Check N: Did you explain each note clearly and accurately?

Check O: Did you use your own sentences?

Check SP: Did you write every sentence so it has a subject and a predicate?

Check CP: Did you begin each sentence with a capital and end with a period?

Check S: Did you correctly spell all the words in the notes and in the word list?

Make a box for each check.

☐ N   ☐ O   ☐ SP   ☐ CP   ☐ S

INDEPENDENT WORK

B Rewrite this passage. Each sentence has one error.

They opened a new mall. We went to it with Jerry and his mother laughed the whole time. There were lots of clowns who gave away balloons. Jerry thought we have too many balloons. We we're getting dizzy from blowing them up. One balloon kept losing it's air.

END OF LESSON 77

A Write a passage answering the question about Side Effects. Use the outline diagram to write your passage.

Question

What are some important things that Mr. Mosely did not know about himself?

Outline Diagram

Mr. Mosely did not know important things about himself. One thing he didn't know was that _____ . Another thing he didn't know was that

_____ .

Check OD: Did you follow the outline diagram exactly?

Check 2T: Did you tell 2 things that Mr. Mosely didn't know?

Check P: Did you correctly punctuate your sentences?

Check VT: Did you always use the past tense to tell what happened?

▨ OD   ▨ 2T   ▨ P   ▨ VT

B Rewrite each sentence so it uses one of the new vocabulary words you've learned.

1. Four workers got tired of quarreling.
2. The trail was long and difficult.
3. The police broke up a quarrel.

INDEPENDENT WORK

C Rewrite each sentence by moving part of the predicate to make the sentence clear.

1. Tammy's father told us about all the songs Tammy learned after Tammy came home from camp.
2. We learned about the longest war in yesterday's reading period.
3. Ms. Delgado told us the story of a puppet who got a longer nose every time he told a lie in the lunchroom.

END OF LESSON 78

A TAKE NOTES AND WRITE ORGANIZED PASSAGE

Vocabulary:	arctic	North Pole	area
	region	lemmings	scarce
	plentiful	invisible	rodents
	pattern	laying	chicks
	frozen		

The snowy owl lives in the cold arctic region near the North Pole. No trees grow in this area. The ground stays frozen all year round. During most of the year, the ground is covered with snow.

Not many animals live in this region; however, lemmings live here. Lemmings are the main food the snowy owl eats. Lemmings are small rodents that are scarce during some years and plentiful during others.

The snowy owl has adapted to the arctic in two main ways. First, the snowy owl is white, so it is almost invisible when it is standing on the snow. The other adaptation of the snowy owl is its pattern for laying eggs. It lays one egg. Several days later, it lays another egg. The chick that is born first is bigger than the other chick. If lemmings are scarce, the older chick takes all the food. The younger chick dies. If lemmings are plentiful, both chicks live.

These are important adaptations that help the snowy owl survive in a very difficult and unfriendly environment.

Environment   Adaptation

Check M: Did you state the main idea in the first sentence and in the conclusion?

Check P: Did you write more than one paragraph?

Check CS: Did you write complete sentences and punctuate them correctly?

Check O: Did you use your own sentences?

Check S: Did you correctly spell all the words that are in the vocabulary box and in your notes?

Make a box for each check.

■ M   ■ P   ■ CS   ■ O   ■ S

Passage 1

Jenny said, "Your problem is that you do not **adapt** to new situations."

George said, "I do too **adapt.** The first time I gave a speech in class, I had a lot of trouble, but now I can do it with no problem at all."

"No," Jenny said, "I don't mean **adapt** to schoolwork. You don't **adapt** well in getting along with other people."

"I do too **adapt** well. When I forgot my lunch, I **adapted** and ate Tina's lunch."

"That's not **adapting** well," Jenny said. "You want everyone to adjust to your needs. You don't adjust to what other people need or feel. You are especially weak at **adapting** when people criticize you."

George started to jump up and down. He shouted, "That's a lie, and you're a liar. Everybody knows that I can adjust to any situation, especially to taking criticism."

1. What part of speech is **adapt?**
2. What does **adapt** probably mean?
3. According to the dictionary, what does **adapt** mean?

Passage 2

They watched the brightly colored birds disappear before their eyes. As soon as the birds landed in the field, they became invisible. Mrs. Brown pointed out, "Their coloring **conceals** the birds when they are on the ground."

Donna said, "Those birds are so well **concealed** that I can't even see them anymore."

Anthony said, "It's impossible for birds with such bright coloring to be **concealed** in a field that is brown and green."

Just then the birds took off. Mrs. Brown said, "The birds are not **concealed** now. They are easily seen."

1. What part of speech is **conceal?**
2. What does **conceal** probably mean?
3. According to the dictionary, what does **conceal** mean?

END OF LESSON 79

A | TAKE NOTES AND WRITE ORGANIZED PASSAGE

Vocabulary:	creatures	challenges	temperatures	survive
	air conditioners	substance	special	crystals
	penguins	blubber	huddle	protect
	cactus	underground	drink	water
	burrows			

Adapting to Extreme Environments

Living creatures survive in all types of environments. Each environment creates different challenges for animals that live there. Some living creatures survive in the South Pole, where temperatures are usually minus 55 degrees. Other living creatures survive in the hot, dry desert, where humans have trouble surviving without air conditioners and deep water wells.

Icefish and penguins that live at the South Pole have adapted to temperatures that are far below freezing. The icefish has a special substance in its blood that keeps ice crystals from forming inside its body. Penguins have thick layers of fat, or blubber, to help them stay warm. Penguins also huddle together to protect each other from cold winds.

Lizards, snakes, and owls live in the hot, dry desert. Lizards and snakes have adapted to their environment by living in burrows. In the daytime, they stay underground out of the hot sun. Owls have nests in the top of cactus plants. The cactus has roots that soak up water quickly when it rains. The cactus can hold that water for a very long time. The owl can peck into the cactus and drink water.

Arctic chill or desert sun is a difficult environment that makes it hard for people to survive. But many plants and animals have adapted so they can live in these extreme environments.

Check M: Did you state the main idea in the first sentence and in the conclusion?

Check P: Did you write more than one paragraph?

Check CS: Did you write complete sentences and punctuate them correctly?

Check O: Did you use your own sentences?

Check S: Did you correctly spell all the words in the notes and in the vocabulary box?

M ☐   P ☐   CS ☐   O ☐   S ☐

END OF LESSON 80

A FIND PRONUNCIATION AND MEANING

1. cerebration
2. cerebration
3. trivia

B Write a sentence using the word <u>cerebration</u> and the word <u>trivia</u>.

1. Write a sentence that uses the word **cerebration.**
2. Write a sentence that uses the word **trivia.**

C DRAW INFERENCES FROM LITERARY TEXTS

What did Ann do that was courageous?

Outline diagram
Ann did something that required courage. [Describe what Ann did.]

Check OD: Did you follow the outline diagram exactly?

Check 4S: Did you write at least 4 sentences?

Check P: Did you punctuate your sentences correctly?

☐ **OD**   ☐ **4S**   ☐ **P**

INDEPENDENT WORK

D **Write the more precise word to replace the underlined part.**

concealed	arduous	monotonous	cajoled
inundated	expunge	altercated	adapt

1. She didn't want to enter the race, but Al <u>persuaded</u> her by reminding her of the many times she had won.

2. Mary tried to <u>remove</u> sad thoughts from her mind.

3. The baseball glove was <u>hidden</u> behind the bedroom door.

4. Those boys <u>argued</u> for over 20 minutes.

5. His dad loved to tell stories about his fishing experiences, but those stories were <u>very boring</u>.

6. The rain <u>flooded</u> the barn and everything in it.

7. That horse can't <u>adjust</u> to his new home.

8. Going up Rock Point was the most <u>difficult</u> climb they had ever attempted.

END OF LESSON 81

A Follow the outline diagram to write about the problem with the argument.

Item A: 1. The teacher gave everybody a high grade in writing.
2. 90% of the class got an F in writing.

Item B: 1. Mr. Jones left work at 5 p.m.
2. When he got home, it was 4:45 p.m.

Outline Diagram

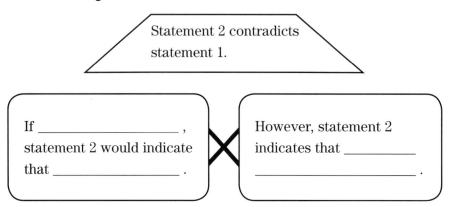

Statement 2 contradicts statement 1.

If _____ , statement 2 would indicate that _____ .

However, statement 2 indicates that _____ _____ .

B FIND PRONUNCIATION AND MEANING

1. concatenate
2. condescending

C Write a sentence for each item.

1. Write a sentence that uses the word **concatenate, concatenating,** or **concatenated.**
2. Write a sentence that uses the word **condescending.**

Statement: Ann was afraid of failing the test for becoming a firefighter.

Quote that provides the evidence: She felt that she was too weak to take the test. She was going to tell the committee that she had decided not to take the test.

Outline Diagram

The statement about Ann is true. [Write the true statement.] The evidence is in paragraph 2. [Write sentences that tell what happened before the quote.] The story continues: "[Copy the quote exactly.]"

Check OD: Did you follow the outline diagram exactly?

Check EQ: Did you give enough information to explain the quote?

Check Q: Did you copy the quote exactly?

Check P: Did you correctly punctuate the quote?

Check S: Did you correctly spell all the words given?

☐ OD   ☐ EQ   ☐ Q   ☐ P   ☐ S

END OF LESSON 82

A FIND PRONUNCIATION AND MEANING

1. stevedore
2. phlegm

B Write a sentence for each item.

1. Write a sentence that uses the word **stevedore.**
2. Write a sentence that uses the word **phlegm.**

C DRAW EVIDENCE TO SUPPORT ANALYSIS AND REFLECTION

Statement: Al did not follow the coach's training program.

Quote that provides the evidence: He didn't do all the things that the coach talked about—none of the wind sprints, the weight training, the dieting, and what the coach called serious hill climbing.

Outline Diagram

The statement about Al is true. [Write the true statement.] The evidence is in paragraph 3. [Write sentences that tell what happened before the quote.] The story continues: "[Copy the quote exactly.]"

Check OD: Did you follow the outline diagram exactly?

Check EQ: Did you give enough information to explain the quote?

Check Q: Did you copy the quote exactly?

Check P: Did you correctly punctuate the quote?

Check S: Did you correctly spell all the words given?

☐ OD   ☐ EQ   ☐ Q   ☐ P   ☐ S

Write a paragraph about the contradiction in item A.

Item A: 1. The teacher gave everybody a high grade in writing.
2. 90% of the class got an F in writing.

Outline Diagram

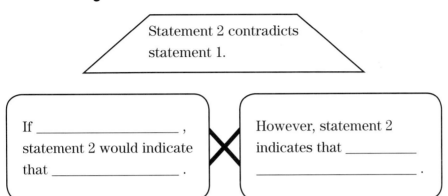

Statement 2 contradicts statement 1.

If _____ , statement 2 would indicate that _____ .

However, statement 2 indicates that _____ _____ .

END OF LESSON 83

A WRITE INFORMATIVE TEXT

Source 1:

Starlings and Sparrows Threaten Bluebird Population

By Sam Dodge, University of Mountain State

Bluebirds are disappearing from North America. The reason is the increased population of sparrows and starlings. Starlings are not native to North America. Sparrows and starlings like to nest in the same places that bluebirds nest. Bluebirds are mild-mannered, peaceful animals, so the frisky sparrows and starlings drive the bluebirds out and take over their nests, even eating their eggs.

Source 2:

Bluebirds Lose Nests

By Lily Mack, Birding Society

Bluebirds are disappearing from North America. They have always preferred to nest in old fence posts and rotting trees near farms and on the outskirts of towns. As our cities grow larger, most rotten trees are cut down, and metal fence posts have largely replaced the old wooden kind. The lack of proper nesting places is the major reason for the decline in the number of bluebirds.

Your passage:

The Disappearance of Bluebirds from North America

Check M: Did you state the main idea in the first sentence and in the conclusion?

Check P: Did you write more than one paragraph?

Check CS: Did you write complete sentences that are correctly punctuated?

Check So: Did you list the author's name and the title for each of your sources at the end of your report?

Check O: Did you use your own sentences?

Check S: Did you correctly spell all the words that are in your notes?

■ **M**   ■ **P**   ■ **CS**   ■ **So**   ■ **O**   ■ **S**

END OF LESSON 84

A   Write about the contradiction.

1. Jack has one sibling.
2. He gets along well with his twin sisters.

Outline Diagram

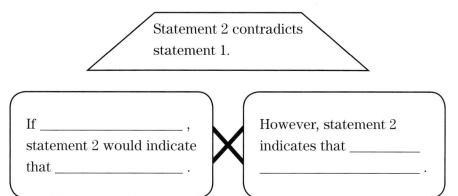

Statement 2 contradicts statement 1.

If _____ , statement 2 would indicate that _____ .

However, statement 2 indicates that _____ _____ .

B   SUPPORT INFERENCES FROM LITERARY TEXT

Statement: Mr. Mosely thought that killing innocent birds was evil.

Outline Diagram

The statement about Mr. Mosely is true. [Write the true statement.] The evidence is in paragraph __. [Write sentences that tell what happened before the quote.] The story continues: "[Copy the quote exactly.]"

Check OD: Did you follow the outline diagram exactly?

Check EQ: Did you give enough information to explain the quote?

Check Q: Did you copy the quote exactly?

Check P: Did you correctly punctuate the quote?

Check S: Did you correctly spell all the words given?

   ☐ OD   ☐ EQ   ☐ Q   ☐ P   ☐ S

END OF LESSON 85

A WRITE INFORMATIVE TEXT

Source 1

The Importance of Bumblebees
by Dr. Justin Chang

Bumblebees are important for agriculture because they transfer pollen from flower to flower. When pollen moves among the flowers in a field, the flowers produce more seeds. More seeds make a bigger crop for farmers.

Bumblebees gather pollen to feed their young. Bumblebees have round bodies covered in soft hair, or fuzz. Pollen sticks to the fuzz as the bee goes from flower to flower. Bumblebees also gather nectar the same way their relatives, honeybees, do. Bumblebees store nectar in their nest.

The bumblebee has other adaptations that help it to be more effective in gathering nectar and pollen. The bumblebee has an extra-long tongue to collect nectar from flowers shaped like tubes. The bumblebee's legs are covered with sticky hairs that help collect pollen. Bumblebees have pockets on the outside of each back leg, called pollen baskets. The baskets are shiny when empty and yellow or red when full of pollen.

Source 2

Bumblebee Behavior
by Edith Rogers

Bumblebees are social insects that form colonies with a single queen. Bumblebee colonies are smaller than those of honeybees, with as few as 50 bumblebees in a nest.

Bumblebees don't have voices, but they have adapted to other means of communication. Bumblebees tell other bees when they have found flowers by running. The bee that has found flowers returns to the hive and runs around inside the hive. The faster the bee runs, the better the place is that the bee has found. Other bees then follow the excited bee to the flowers.

Your report:

The Adaptations of the Bumblebee

Check M: Did you state the main idea in the introduction and in the conclusion?

Check P: Did you write more than one paragraph?

Check CS: Did you write complete sentences and correctly punctuate them?

Check So: At the end of your report, did you list the author's name and the title for each of your sources?

Check S: Did you correctly spell all the words from your notes?

☐ M   ☐ P   ☐ CS   ☐ So   ☐ S

END OF LESSON 86

A GRAMMAR CONVENTIONS

Here are some prepositions that you've worked with:

about	behind	from	over	after
in	to	at	beside	near
through	around	by	of	under
before	for	on	with	

B Write two sentences about each picture. Use prepositions in your sentences.

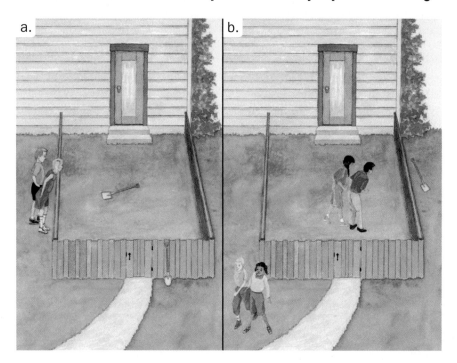

a.

b.

INDEPENDENT WORK

C Complete each sentence with a colorful expression.

1. Roberto felt as free ▮▮▮▮▮▮▮▮▮▮▮ .

2. Even though she was 95, her mind was as sharp as ▮▮▮▮▮▮▮▮▮▮ .

3. Sy's car was as old as ▮▮▮▮▮▮▮▮▮▮ .

4. His face was as white as ▮▮▮▮▮▮▮▮ .

END OF LESSON 87

A FIX EVIDENCE BY ADDING ONLY

You've worked with faulty arguments. The conclusion that a faulty argument draws is not the **only** conclusion that is possible.

You can fix faulty arguments by **changing the evidence.** When you change the evidence, you create a whole new argument, but the new argument has the evidence a person would need to draw the conclusion of the original argument.

Here's a faulty argument:

The big clock always chimes at 10 p.m.

I hear the big clock chiming. Therefore, it must be 10 p.m.

That conclusion is not the only one that's possible.

If the argument presented **different** evidence, we could safely draw the conclusion that it is 10 p.m.

B Rewrite the more general evidence so it uses the word <u>only</u>.

1. Every time Amy's mother goes to Z-Mart, she spends a lot of money.
   Amy's mother spent a lot of money yesterday.
   Therefore, she must have gone to Z-Mart.

2. Mario always tracks dirt into the kitchen.
   There are dirt tracks on the kitchen floor.
   Therefore, Mario tracked that dirt into the kitchen.

3. Lina always gets sick after she travels to Texas.
   Lina is very sick.
   Therefore, she must have traveled to Texas recently.

Write two sentences about each picture. Use prepositions in your sentences.

a.

b.

INDEPENDENT WORK

D **Rewrite each long sentence as two or more smaller sentences. Remove the word *and*.**

1. We went to the fair and we rode the rides and we had popcorn.
2. Mr. Marcelli made the posters and Tricia decorated the room and Benny took the tickets.
3. The village is more than 500 years old and it is in the mountains and it is hard to get to.

END OF LESSON 88

A WRITE INFORMATIVE TEXT

Source 1

Honeybee Communication
by Gabe Berg

Honeybees have a waggle dance that is much fancier than a bumblebee's. A bumblebee runs in the hive to indicate how many good flowers the bee has found. The faster the bumblebee runs, the more flowers there are. The honeybee's waggle dance gives detailed information about where food can be found. The dance indicates the direction of the flowers, how far the flowers are from the hive, and what kind of flowers they are.

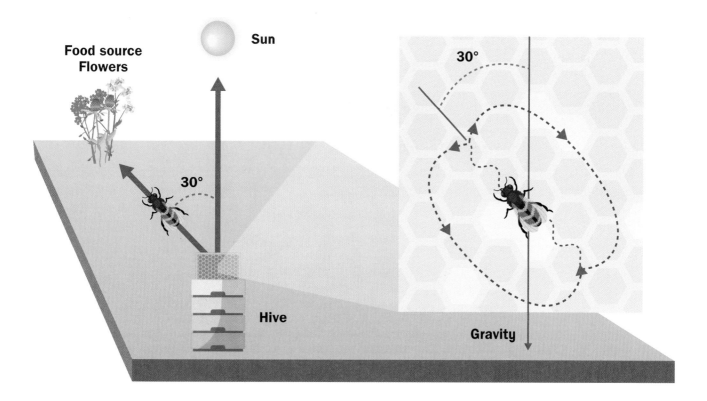

The honeybee walks in a figure 8 to do the waggle dance. First, the bee moves at an angle to indicate the direction of the flowers. The angle is referenced to the sun. Straight up is toward the sun; straight down is away from the sun. The angle she moves between straight up and straight down indicates the direction of the flowers. Second, the faster the bee waggles, the further away the flowers are. She indicates the kind of flowers by the scent of the pollen she carries on her legs.

Research on Bee Movement
by Isabel Sanchez

Karl von Frisch first discovered the waggle dance in the 1940s. He placed two bee feeders at different distances and in different directions from a bee hive. The bees from the hives found the feeders. Frisch put a spot of paint on the backs of bees as they visited the feeder. The bees at one feeder got a pink spot. The bees at the other feeder got a blue spot. After he colored many bees at the feeders, he went back to the hive. He watched the bees carefully. He saw that all the bees with a blue spot danced the same way; all the bees with a pink spot danced the same way. However, the dance of the blue bees was different from the dance of the pink bees. Then Frisch repeated the experiment, placing the feeders in different directions and at different distances. This information showed him how to interpret the waggle dance.

Modern scientists are studying more about bees. These bee scientists try different ways to track the movements of insects. One tracking method was to glue a little radio on the insect's back with superglue. Each insect with a radio backpack sends a signal to the scientists. The radio has been used successfully with dragonflies and large insects. However, when scientists stuck the radio on a bumblebee, the bumblebee couldn't fly. The bumblebee was too small to carry the transmitter.

Source 3: Watch a video illustrating the waggle dance.

(Find a video illustrating the waggle dance and possibly one that explains how scientists learned what the waggle dance means.)

Your passage:

The Waggle Dance of the Honeybee

Honeybees do a waggle dance to tell other bees where food can be found. The waggle dance is based on a figure 8.

Check M: Did you state the main idea in the introduction and in the conclusion?

Check P: Did you write more than one paragraph?

Check CP: Did you write complete sentences and correctly punctuate them?

Check So: Did you name the sources?

Check S: Did you correctly spell all the words from your notes?

◻ **M**   ◻ **P**   ◻ **CP**   ◻ **So**   ◻ **S**

B **Rewrite the more general evidence so it uses the word <u>only</u>.**

1. That picture has a lot of blue in it.
   Linda makes pictures that have a lot of blue in them.
   Therefore, Linda must have made that picture.

2. Watchdogs keep burglars away from houses.
   Burglars never go to Mr. Lam's house.
   Therefore, Mr. Lam must have a watchdog.

3. Jim always wears striped shirts.
   That person in the distance is wearing a striped shirt.
   Therefore, that person must be Jim.

END OF LESSON 89

A PROVERBS

Here are some proverbs:

1. The best things in life are free.
2. The grass is always greener on the other side of the fence.

1   2   3

1. a. Who thinks that the grass is greener on the other side of the fence?
   b. Explain your answer.

2. The best things in life are free. Name one of these things.

B FIX EVIDENCE BY ADDING ALL OR EVERY

You've worked with faulty arguments. You changed the evidence by using the word **only** and created a new argument that drew the conclusion the original argument drew.

Some faulty arguments are different. To make it possible to draw the conclusion that argument draws, you use the words **all** or **every** in the evidence.

Here's an argument of that type:

> **Tadpoles live in ponds.**
>
> **I see a pond.**
>
> **Therefore, it must have tadpoles in it.**

C Change one of the sentences in the evidence so it draws the conclusion that is given. Use the word all or every.

1. Many people who wear Craddy running shoes run faster.
   J. J. Terry wears Craddy running shoes.
   Therefore, J. J. must be running faster than he did.

2. Liver is a food that contains iron.
   You should eat foods that contain iron.
   Therefore, you should eat liver.

3. George has lots of tools.
   A level is a tool.
   Therefore, George has a level.

INDEPENDENT WORK

D **The map and the statement contradict each other. You don't know whether the map is accurate or the statement is accurate. Tell about the contradiction.**

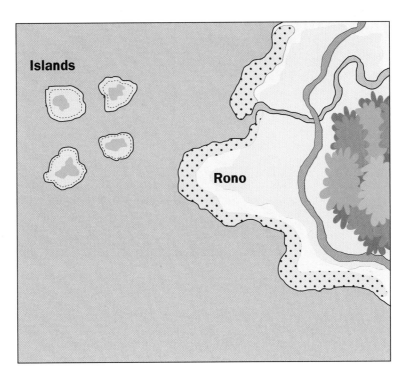

Statement: The islands off the coast of Rono form a triangle.

Outline Diagram

The map contradicts

_____ .

If _____ ,
The map would show _____
_____ .

However, the map
_____
_____ .

E **Write two sentences about each picture. Use prepositions in your sentences.**

a.

b.

A Fix the evidence in these arguments by rewriting one sentence. Add the word <u>all</u> or <u>every</u>.

Argument 1:

Mrs. Jones has lots of jewelry.
An emerald necklace is a type of jewelry.
Therefore, Mrs. Jones must have an emerald necklace.

Argument 2:

Radiator hoses are parts of cars.
Many parts of Bumpo cars are excellent.
Therefore, Bumpos must have excellent radiator hoses.

Argument 3:

You should do exercises to improve your endurance.
Running 30 miles every week improves your endurance.
Therefore, you should run 30 miles every week.

B WRITE INFORMATIVE TEXT

Source 1

Facts about the Honeybee Brain

by Lori Abel

Honeybees are very smart. The honeybee brain is about the size of a sesame seed. Their small brains are able to make very complicated calculations in order to find their way using the sun as a reference. The sun moves constantly, so keeping track of where the bee is also requires keeping track of the changes in the sun's position. The honeybee brain can figure out about 10 trillion calculations in one second. Most computers can figure 16 billion calculations in one second. That means the honeybee brain is 625 times faster than most computers.

Honeybees have a remarkable ability to learn and recall things. Bees can learn colors. Scientists in Australia showed bees a color that indicated a specific path in a maze. The bees were able to find their way through the maze because they recognized the color.

The Green Brain Project
by Alan Dodge

The Green Brain Project in Britain is building a robot that thinks, senses, and acts like a honeybee. Bee brains are much smaller than other brains and yet extremely intelligent. Bees' brains have far fewer connections than other animal brains and yet accomplish so much with those few connections. Using a bee brain model, scientists expect to get more intelligence with less effort. The bee's ability to find its way so efficiently is especially important for drone bees. The bee's sense of smell is so precise that a drone with that sense of smell could detect poisonous gases. With the ability of a bee to track direction with only the sun as a guide, the drone could precisely identify the location of the danger. What the bee does with its brain is also highly relevant to what is needed for drone behavior.

The Green Brain Project has transferred the bee's sense of smell and sense of direction to computer robots called drones, with partial success. This first step is very promising. With further study, scientists will create drones that have the same behavior bees have.

Source 3: Watch a video about the Green Brain Project.

(Find a video about the Green Brain Project and honeybees.)

Your passage:

Bee Brain Robots

Check I: Did you state the main idea in the introduction and in the conclusion?

Check P: Did you write more than one paragraph?

Check CS: Did you write complete sentences and correctly punctuate them?

Check So: At the end of your report, did you list the author's name and the title for each of your sources?

Check S: Did you correctly spell all the words from your notes?

■ I   ■ P   ■ CS   ■ So   ■ S

INDEPENDENT WORK

C **Rewrite this passage. Remove the <u>and</u>'s. Fix the contractions and make one sentence clear by moving part of the predicate. Correct any wrong word.**

The girls in our class went to the White River and we collected rocks and some of them were beautiful. Edna and Lisa had the mostest beautiful rocks and there rocks was red and white. We talked a lot about how to find good rocks on the plane trip home.

D **Write four sentences that use prepositional phrases. You may write about the picture, or you may make up your sentences.**

1. ███████████████████████████████

2. ███████████████████████████████

3. ███████████████████████████████

4. ███████████████████████████████

END OF LESSON 91

A Write the answers to the questions.

1. A baseball team is like a chain. How many links are in the chain?
2. If each player does his or her job well, how many weak links does the chain have?
3. If 3 players do not do their job well, how many weak links does the chain have?

B Follow the outline diagram to explain the contradiction in Teeny's report.

Teeny's Report

A guy stopped me and made me take my brand new coat off. That guy put the coat on and left. I didn't try to stop him. That guy was at least twice as big as I am.

Outline Diagram

Teeny contradicted himself.

If _____
_____ ,
Teeny's last statement would indicate
that _____ .

However, Teeny's last statement
indicates that _____
_____ .

C Add the word <u>all</u>, <u>every</u>, or <u>only</u> to one sentence in the evidence to make the evidence lead to the conclusion.

Rosa's Argument:

Millionaires have lots of possessions.
Mrs. Anderson has lots of possessions.
Therefore, Mrs. Anderson must be a millionaire.

Tia's Argument:

Becky is a good basketball player.
Good players are on our school's basketball team.
Therefore, Becky must be on our school's basketball team.

Moka's Argument:

Redwood trees grow in California.
Sandy saw a redwood tree growing.
Therefore, she was in California.

D Follow the outline diagram to tell about the problem with each argument.

Outline Diagram

| _____ concludes that _____ _____ _____ . | ✕ | _____ does not indicate that _____[all/only]____ _____ . | = | Therefore, _____ _____ might _____ or _____ . |

Tado's Argument Trucks have tires.
The vehicle in our garage has tires.
Therefore, the vehicle in our garage must be a truck.

Tado **concludes that** the vehicle in our garage is a truck. However, the evidence **does not indicate that** trucks are the **only** vehicles that have tires. **Therefore,** the vehicle in our garage **might** be a motorcycle **or** tricycle.

Mia's Argument:

There's a dollar in the street.
Billy is always losing money.
Therefore, that dollar must belong to Billy.

Dot's Argument:

There's an animal sitting in that tree.
Birds sit in trees.
Therefore, that animal must be a bird.

INDEPENDENT WORK

E **Rewrite each sentence. Replace the underlined words with a more precise word. Use a thesaurus to help you.**

1. When she saw her report card, she was <u>not elated</u>.

2. The suggestion to take your raincoat to the game was <u>not silly</u>.

3. The street food was <u>not nice</u>.

F **Write four sentences that use prepositional phrases. You may write about the picture, or you may make up your sentences.**

1. ████████████████████████████████

2. ████████████████████████████████

3. ████████████████████████████████

4. ████████████████████████████████

END OF LESSON 92

A Follow the outline diagram to explain the contradiction in Laura's report.

Laura's Report

I was heading west on Route 6. The sun was in my eyes, and I couldn't see the road. I went off the road at 7 a.m.

Outline Diagram

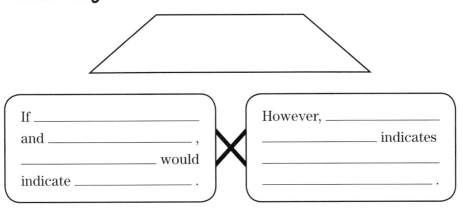

If _____
and _____ ,
_____ would
indicate _____ .

However, _____
_____ indicates
_____
_____ .

B Rewrite each item by joining the sentences with one of these words: *and, or, but.*

> The dog was small. It was very tough.
> The dog was small, **but** it was very tough.

1. She was tired. She kept working.
2. The car was old. It had a flat tire.
3. She will go to a movie. She will listen to a CD.
4. The sun came up. The birds started to sing.
5. She must save her money. She will not be able to buy the bike.
6. They had to practice. They were very tired.
7. The wind blew. The trees bent.
8. The car looked good. It did not perform well.

Follow the outline diagram to tell about the problem with the argument.

Sao's Argument:

Hammers are tools that have no moving parts.
Uncle Bill has a tool that has no moving parts.
Therefore, Uncle Bill has a hammer.

Sunny's Argument:

Days that are warm and sunny occur in spring.
April 3 is a day in spring.
Therefore, April 3 will be warm and sunny.

Ron's Argument:

Plants need sunlight to live.
That plant is dying.
Therefore, that plant must not be getting enough sunlight.

Outline Diagram

| _____ concludes that _____ _____ _____ . | ✕ | However, the evidence does not indicate that _____[all/only]_____ _____ . | = | Therefore, _____ _____ might _____ or _____ . |

INDEPENDENT WORK

Rewrite each sentence with a more familiar or more precise word in place of the underlined word. You can use the dictionary in the back of your textbook, or on the internet.

1. A miniscule amount of powder was on the floor.

2. The two forces were equipollent.

END OF LESSON 93

A **Rewrite each item by joining the sentences with one of these words: *and*, *or*, *but*.**

1. I need to study hard. I won't pass the test.
2. Her feet feel cold. It is not cold in the room.
3. The mountain was steep. It was covered with deep snow.
4. He will have to be careful. He will fall.
5. The horse was very smart. He didn't always do what his master ordered him to do.

B **Follow the outline diagram to tell about the problem in each of these arguments.**

Julio's Argument:

Jamal always tracks dirt into the kitchen.
Dirt tracks are in the kitchen.
Therefore, Jamal must have made those dirt tracks.

Penny's Argument:

That picture has a lot of blue in it.
Linda makes pictures with a lot of blue.
Linda must have made that picture.

Outline Diagram

_____ concludes that _____ _____ _____ .

However, the evidence does not indicate that [all/only] _____ _____ .

= Therefore, _____ _____ or _____ might _____ .

C Follow the outline diagram to write about the contradiction in Blinky's account.

Blinky's account

I left work at 5 p.m. It takes me 30 minutes to get home. When I got home, I saw two men sneaking around the house. So I called the police at 5:15 p.m.

Outline Diagram

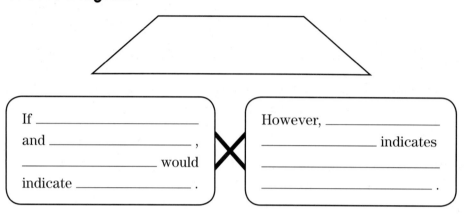

If _____
and _____ ,
_____ would
indicate _____ .

However, _____
_____ indicates
_____
_____ .

D Rewrite each sentence with a familiar synonym for the unfamiliar word. You can use the thesaurus in the back of your textbook, or on the Internet.

1. His plan for raising money was circuitous.
2. Many of the things she observed were ambiguous.

END OF LESSON 94

A PLAN AND WRITE AN OPINION WITH SUPPORTING EVIDENCE

Question: What is your opinion about homework?

Source 1

Too Much Homework, Not Enough Time
by Toby Laxton, Cougarville Middle School

In my opinion, middle school students have too much homework. With the current emphasis on passing standards, teachers are trying to get us to learn more by doing more homework. There are many problems with having too much homework.

Teachers often have students learning material at home that was not discussed in class at all. The teacher reasons that there isn't enough time to cover all the material necessary for the standards, so lots of homework is necessary. That means students end up learning from a piece of paper instead of from an actual human being. The teacher is better to learn from because the teacher can see when students don't understand and can explain the concepts better than a piece of paper can. All the time students spend on homework is often wasted, because it is time spent in frustration, misunderstanding, and writing down wrong answers.

Another problem with too much homework is that many students just simply give up and don't do the homework. Consequently, their grades go down, and they just quit school, even if they still attend classes because their parents and the system force them to attend. They quit mentally.

The amount of homework that teachers give is often ridiculous and accomplishes nothing. Homework doesn't mean that students learn more. Many students end up with lower grades, more frustration, more hatred of school, and less desire to further their education.

Source 2

The Overall Effectiveness of Homework
by Sadie Thomas
University of the Coast

Three types of studies have examined the effects of homework on academic achievement. One type of study compares students who receive homework assignments with students who don't receive any homework. These studies show that homework for high school students had twice the positive effect that homework for middle school students has and four times the effect that homework for elementary students has.

Another type of study compares homework to in-class supervised study. For elementary students, in-class study results in better achievement. The supervision by teachers who know the expectations makes in-class supervised study much more effective than homework.

The third type of study compares the amount of homework students report doing with their achievement scores. For students in elementary grades, doing more homework made no difference in grades. For middle or junior-high students, doing more homework made only a small difference, with students who do more homework getting only slightly better grades. For high school students, doing more homework helped improve grades a moderate amount.

In conclusion, homework is more effective for students in high school. For middle school and especially for elementary students, homework has little or no value.

Source 3

Effective Homework Assignments
by Dr. Elsworth Higgins
Big Town College

Homework can have positive or negative effects on learning. The amount of time spent on homework is less important than the quality of the homework. Shorter and more frequent homework assignments are more effective than longer but fewer assignments. Assignments that involve review are more effective than assignments that cover only material taught in class that day.

Older students and students doing well in school gain more by doing homework. Students who are struggling need more support when doing independent work, so homework for them is not a good idea. Homework policies should give individual teachers the flexibility to take into account the unique needs and circumstances of their students to maximize positive effects and minimize negative ones.

Planning Your Opinion Paper:

Opinion Statement

Reason 1

Reason 2

Reason 3

Here are some ideas for opinion statements:

1. I think that children should not start doing homework until age 10.
2. I believe that children in grade 4 should have no more than one hour of homework every night.
3. I think that no one should have to do homework.

Check M: Did you state your main idea in the first sentence and in the conclusion?

Check CS: Did you write complete sentences that are correctly punctuated?

Check P: Did you write more than one paragraph?

Check So: Did you tell the source for details you use?

Check O: Did you use your own sentences?

Check S: Did you correctly spell all the words that are given?

■ **M**　　　■ **CS**　　　■ **P**　　　■ **So**　　　■ **O**　　　■ **S**

B **Write the number of each situation and the letter of the proverb that fits.**

Proverbs	Situations
A. Practice makes perfect.	1. Andy thinks that Jill's job is better than his. Jill thinks that Andy's job is better than hers.
B. The best things in life are free.	2. The first four times Tom grilled burgers, they were either too raw or they were burnt. By the end of the summer, his burgers were great.
C. The grass is always greener on the other side of the fence.	
D. A chain is no stronger than its weakest link.	
E. The early bird catches the worm.	
F. Practice what you preach.	

3.  This is wonderful.

4.  Don't break the law.

5.

6.  I get the front seat.

C **Write combined sentences for all the items.**

> **Hint =** The dog was small, but it was very tough.
>
> I can go to the store, or I can watch TV.
>
> Mr. Green runs every morning, and he walks every evening.

1. We went on vacation. We had a wonderful time.
2. Garrett closed the car door. He forgot to lock it.
3. The dog has to be fenced. He will bite the mail carrier.
4. Roberto worked on the car all day. The car still did not run.

INDEPENDENT WORK

D **Find the appropriate outline diagram in the back of your textbook and write about the problem with Hilda's account.**

Hilda's account:

I have three sisters. All are older than I am. Ellen is the oldest. Diana is the youngest. She was very small when she was a baby. I remember seeing her just after she was born. She looked like a tiny doll. You would not believe how big she is now.

END OF LESSON 95

A Write the letter of the proverb that matches the numbered situation.

Proverbs	Situations
A. Practice makes perfect.	1. The man yelled at Bob and Dan, "Don't talk so loud!"
B. The best things in life are free.	2. Kathy went fishing every day last summer. In the first two weeks, she caught five little fish. During the last week of summer, she caught 12 big fish.
C. The grass is always greener on the other side of the fence.	3. Grandma was so happy when the kids came over and told her how much they loved her.
D. A chain is no stronger than its weakest link.	4. Sally went out first for the Easter egg hunt. By the time the other children went out, Sally had found all the eggs.
E. The early bird catches the worm.	5. Joe would rather go to Karen's school, and Karen would rather go to Joe's school.
F. Practice what you preach.	6.

B WRITE A STORY WITH A PARALLEL THEME

Which sentence <u>best</u> describes the lesson that Ann learns in this story?

1. Ann learns to relax and take it easy.
2. Ann learns to control her nerves.
3. Ann learns that she can pass the firefighter test.
4. Ann learns that if she works hard to achieve her goal, she will achieve it.

Theme: If you keep working hard to achieve your goal in spite of failure, you will achieve your goal.

Your story:

Marta wanted so badly to become a lifeguard. The last time she took the test, she failed because she could not pull the victim from the bottom of the pool fast enough to start CPR within 3 minutes. She had a hard time getting the heavy victim out of the water and onto the deck.

Check WH: Did Marta keep working hard to achieve her goal?

Check SB: Did Marta face some setbacks?

Check E: Did Marta achieve her goal in the end?

Check QM: Did you punctuate your sentences correctly and use quote marks for things people said?

      ☐ **WH**   ☐ **SB**   ☐ **E**   ☐ **QM**

C Write about the problem with Fran's statements.

Here's what Fran said:

Mrs. Johnson fixes wonderful chicken and makes great pizzas. She's going to fix a stew for us. I know it will be wonderful.

Outline Diagram

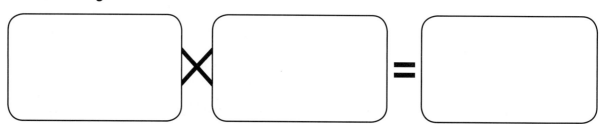

INDEPENDENT WORK

D Use __and__, __but__, __or__ to combine the two sentences in each item.

1. The packers worked all day. They were not too tired to go out with friends that night.
2. Josh was so happy to see his father. He was happy to be finished with school.
3. You need to feed the sheep. Josh will have to do it.
4. I will never finish my homework before ten. I can get up early in the morning to finish it.

END OF LESSON 96

A PLAN AND WRITE AN OPINION WITH SUPPORTING EVIDENCE

Source 1

Ban Pets

by Kevonte Jacobs

Milton Elementary School

In my opinion, people should not have pets. My primary objection to keeping pets is the tremendous amount of money spent caring for animals. We have huge human needs all around us that go unsatisfied. People care more for their dogs than they do for their fellow humans. This gives animal life the same value as human life. Crimes against animals seem to draw greater outrage than crimes against humanity. Cruelty is never acceptable, but an animal life does not have the same value as a human life. Humans should be taken care of before we waste money on pets.

Also, pets tie a family down. You can never leave your home for more than a day. Every time you want to go on vacation, you have to figure out who will feed and take care of your pet while you're gone. You can always leave your pet at a kennel, but that is very expensive.

Source 2

Pets and Health

by NaAsia Smith

Elk Ridge Middle School

I think that people should have pets. Pets are good for a person's health. Research has shown that if people who suffer from various diseases keep pets, they will experience less depression than people who are suffering from similar diseases and don't keep pets.

People with pets get more exercise than people without pets. Dogs need exercise and love to go for walks. So good pet owners take their pet for a walk every day, rain or shine. Other activities related to pets—like feeding, bathing, playing, and cleaning—are also good ways to exercise.

Pets are great companions and prevent loneliness. Pets give you unconditional love and are always faithful. You can tell a pet all your secrets. You know the secrets will be safe with your pet.

Dogs are especially good for safety. Dogs warn against dangers and bark when strangers come to the door. Dogs protect children and other members of their family.

Source 3

Positive Effects of Having Pets
by Dr. Ximena Pritchard
University of the Hills

Scientific studies show that children who grow up with pets have less risk of allergies and asthma. In addition, many children also learn responsibility, compassion, and empathy from having a dog or cat.

Having the love and companionship of a loyal dog can make a child feel important and help him or her develop a positive self-image. Youngsters who are emotionally attached to their dog are better able to build relationships with other people.

Studies have also shown that hyperactive or overly aggressive kids are calmer with a pet around. Of course, both the dog and the child need to be trained to behave appropriately with each other.

Both children and adults can benefit from playing with dogs, which can be a source of calmness and relaxation as well as a source of stimulation for the brain and body.

Question: What is your opinion about kids having pets?

Check M: Did you state your main idea in the first sentence and in the conclusion?

Check CS: Did you write complete sentences that are correctly punctuated?

Check P: Did you write more than one paragraph?

Check So: Did you tell the source for details you use?

Check O: Did you use your own sentences?

Check S: Did you correctly spell all the words that are given?

　■ M　　　■ CS　　　■ P　　　■ So　　　■ O　　　■ S

B USE PRECISE LANGUAGE

Some sentences are called **commands** or **directions**. They tell somebody what to do.

These sentences are strange because they don't have a subject. The first word is usually a verb. It is capitalized.

Here are sentences that give directions:

1. Turn the corner.
2. Put the dog outside.
3. Stop making so much noise.
4. Turn your paper over, and copy the problems.

Write a sentence that tells a person what to do.

C Follow these directions to make figures.

1. Make a square.
   Make a **J** in the square.
   Make a **V** just above the square.

2. Make a square that is 5 inches high.
   Make a J in the middle of the square. Make the J one inch tall.
   Make a V just above the left side of the square. Make the V one inch tall.

INDEPENDENT WORK

D Write about the problem with May's argument.

May's argument: Crickets make noise at night.
   There was a lot of noise last night.
   Therefore, a lot of crickets must have been out last night.

E Combine the sentences using <u>and</u>, <u>or</u>, <u>but</u>.

> The dog was small. It was very tough.
> The dog was small, **but** it was very tough.

1. He wanted to rest. He had to keep working.
2. I can go to the store. I can watch TV.
3. Mr. Green runs every morning. He walks every evening.

END OF LESSON 97

A WRITE A STORY WITH A PARALLEL THEME

Which sentence best describes the lesson that the reader should learn from the story *Side Effects*?

1. Mr. Mosely doesn't know why the birds died.
2. Mr. Mosely is completely unaware of the damaging effects of his actions.
3. Mr. Mosely is a bad gardener.
4. Mr. Mosely blames someone else for the dead birds in his garden.

Theme: People can be completely unaware of the damaging effects of their actions.

Your story:

Farmer John had a big problem with mice. Mice were eating his grain, using the cushions of his tractor for their nests, making nests in the radiator of his truck and car, and leaving droppings everywhere. To solve his mouse problem Farmer John got two cats, Romeo and Juliet, who were excellent mouse cats. However, they were not able to kill all the mice.

Farmer John went to the feed store to talk to Marvin about his mouse problem. He said, "Marvin, how can I get rid of thousands of mice?" Marvin showed him some mouse poison.

Check A: Did your main character do admirable things?

Check DE: Did the admirable deeds involve some damaging effect?

Check B: Did your character see the damage and blame someone else for it?

Check R: Did your character remain unaware that he or she was the cause of the damage?

Check QM: Did you use quote marks for things people say and punctuate your sentences correctly?

Check S: Did you correctly spell all the words that are given?

☐ **A**　　　☐ **DE**　　　☐ **B**　　　☐ **R**　　　☐ **QM**　　　☐ **S**

USE PRECISE LANGUAGE

Make a rectangle that is 3 inches wide.

Make a B just outside the lower corner.

Make a T on the top line of the figure.

Make letters this size: B T

INDEPENDENT WORK

C **Write about the problem with Ana's argument.**

Ana's argument:

Many animals that fly have feathers.
I see a flying animal.
Therefore, it must have feathers.

Outline Diagram

_____ concludes
that _____
_____
_____ .

×

However, the evidence
does not indicate that
_____ [all/only]
_____ .

=

Therefore, _____
_____
or _____ might
_____ .

END OF LESSON 98

A · USE PRECISE LANGUAGE

Make a square.

Make a diagonal line from an upper corner to a lower corner.

Make an R in a triangle.

B · WRITE AN OPINION PIECE

Source 1

Rules for Emotional Support Animals
by Eddy Longfellow, Sheriff

Federal regulations don't identify "emotional support animals" very clearly. Unlike a "service dog," an emotional support animal can be a member of any species, does not have to be trained to do anything, and can be nothing more than your personal pet.

If you want your parrot or pig officially accepted as an emotional support animal, the one requirement is that you have to be under treatment for a mental disorder. And you must obtain a letter from a physician or licensed mental health professional indicating that the animal is necessary for your mental health or treatment for your psychiatric condition. Then you can live with your animal in no-pets housing or take your animal for free on an airplane, as long as you have the letter with you.

Source 2

The Benefits of Emotional Support Animals
by Asa Kudrun, Animal News

People should be allowed to take their pets anywhere. There are numerous studies demonstrating the extensive health benefits for people with pets, whether they are officially an emotional service animal or not.

Examples of proven health benefits include
- lower cholesterol
- lower blood pressure
- lower triglycerides
- reduced stress levels
- reduced feelings of loneliness

- better mental health
- increased activity
- more opportunities for exercise
- more time spent outdoors (for dog owners especially)
- more opportunities for socialization.

Because of all these health benefits, people who love their pets should be able to take them anywhere they go. Allowing people to take their pets anywhere will reduce our healthcare costs.

Source 3

Service Animal Fraud

by Akeesha Daniels, Furryfeed News

Service animal fraud is out of hand. Fraud occurs when owners who are not mentally ill or disabled use phony certificates and "service animal" vests that they bought online. It's not unusual anymore to find all sorts of emotional support livestock in an aircraft cabin, on a bus or train, in a mall or restaurant, and even at museums and sporting venues. Pit bulls, rabbits, monkeys, parrots, turtles, guinea pigs, snakes, and any pet you can name can be seen making a mess most anywhere. These pets are not there because their owners have physical disabilities or crippling emotional needs. They have perfectly healthy owners.

Fraud is so difficult to prevent because businesses who deny access to a legitimate service animal can be fined $55,000 to $100,000. Consequently, most businesses don't ask a lot questions and accept emotional support animals or fake service animals without debate. So we are seeing more monkeys riding in the shopping carts at the local grocery store and more pigs on planes. People should not be allowed to take a pet to any public place.

What is your opinion about emotional support animals?

Check M: Did you state your main idea in the first sentence and in the conclusion?

Check CS: Did you write complete sentences that are correctly punctuated?

Check LP: Did you link your paragraphs with connecting words such as another reason, in addition, because, for instance?

Check So: Did you tell the source for details you use?

Check O: Did you use your own sentences?

Check S: Did you correctly spell all the words that are given?

☐ **M** ☐ **CS** ☐ **LP** ☐ **So** ☐ **O** ☐ **S**

END OF LESSON 99

A USE PRECISE LANGUAGE

First sentence: Tell about the sides of the rectangle.

Second sentence: Tell about the diagonal line.

Third sentence: Tell about the **H.**

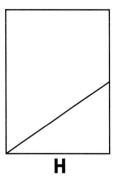

H

B WRITE AN OPINION PIECE

Source 1

The Benefits of Having Children Do Chores
by Maxine Reddin, University of Midtown

I studied whether having children do household chores starting at age 3 or 4 predicted the children's success in their mid-20s. I found that children who had done chores as young children were more likely to be well-adjusted, had better relationships with friends and family, and were more successful in their careers. Getting toddlers started doing chores is really easier than waiting until children are older. Toddlers are eager to please and eager to help with chores. They can start by helping sort clothes. Sorting also teaches children an important skill: How to categorize information.

Parents who missed the boat on starting their children out as toddlers might find it more difficult to get their children on board with a chore list. A key to chore success lies in family participation. Rather than saying, "It's time to do your chores," you can say, "It's time for us to do our chores." Making chore time a fun family event will probably result in more cooperation. You can turn on music and sing while working. Making chores a fun experience will gain more cooperation. Children will continue to feel happy when they do chores.

Facts about Chores for Children
by Liam Long, Brown Research

The benefits of requiring children to do chores starting at a very young age are clear. But despite the benefits, research shows that fewer parents are requiring their children to pitch in. According to a survey we did, 82 percent of grown-ups say they had regular chores when they were growing up, but only 28 percent reported asking their children to do any. Parents said their children were extremely busy with school and extracurricular activities. Parents didn't want to pile more responsibility on them.

Source 3

Getting Chores Done Right or Wrong
by Aleesha Maple, Children's Hospital

Parents often don't ask their children to help with family chores because children don't do the job right. Their children end up going off to college without knowing how to wash their clothes, cook a meal, or even basic things like how to change a lightbulb.

Getting a chore done right the first time is probably an unreasonable expectation. The best way to get chores done right is to do the chore with the child, especially while the child is learning how to do the task. Children may not do the chore correctly the first time, but if a parent continues to do the chore with the child, soon all the parts of doing the chore right will be in place.

Rather than just saying, "Well, you need to dust," you do it with them and show them how to do it and what needs to be done. While taking the time to teach children their chores can initially take longer, investing the time has a huge payoff.

What is your opinion about children doing chores at home?

Check M: Did you state your main idea in the first sentence and in the conclusion?

Check CS: Did you write complete sentences that are correctly punctuated?

Check LP: Did you link your paragraphs with connecting words such as another reason, in addition, because, for instance?

Check So: Did you tell the source for details you use?

Check O: Did you use your own sentences?

Check S: Did you correctly spell all the words that are given?

| ■ M | ■ CS | ■ LP | ■ So | ■ O | ■ S |

END OF LESSON 100

A **Write directions for making this figure.**

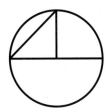

For some directions, you use the words **horizontal, vertical,** and **diagonal**.

Horizontal is from side to side, like the horizon. ——

Vertical is straight up and down. |

Make a [＿＿＿] line from [＿＿＿] to [＿＿＿].

B **Write a story with the same theme as <u>Works and Goals</u>.**

Theme: Listen to the advice of people who have more experience than you.

Story Idea: Tad and Josh were pretty good math students. Tad had a slightly higher score for math daily work than Josh. This was the first class about equations that they had taken. The final test was coming up in 3 weeks. Mr. Ledger, the math teacher, told the students that they would need to study hard for this test. "You'll study better if you study in a quiet place. No music, no distractions," Mr. Ledger advised.

Check B: Did you show how Tad is a little better than Josh?

Check A: Did you describe the advice that Mr. Ledger gives?

Check I: Did you describe what Tad did instead of following good advice?

Check R: Did you describe an event in which Tad regrets that he did not follow the advice?

Check QM: Did you use quote marks for things people said and punctuate your sentences correctly?

Check S: Did you correctly spell all the words that are given?

▪ **B**　　▪ **A**　　▪ **I**　　▪ **R**　　▪ **QM**　　▪ **S**

END OF LESSON 101

A Write your directions for making the figure. Write each part as a separate sentence. Start each sentence with the word <u>draw</u>, <u>make</u>, or <u>shade</u>. Write at least four sentences.

> For some directions, you use the words **horizontal, vertical,** and **diagonal.**
>
> **Horizontal** is from side to side, like the horizon. ▬
>
> **Vertical** is straight up and down.

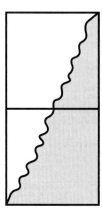

B Combine these pairs of sentences so they end with a noun. Label the part of speech for each word.

> ### Sample Items
>
> a. She was a girl.
>   She was smart.
>
> b. That bird is active.
>   That bird is a rooster.

1. The dinner was delicious. The dinner was a meal.
2. Our trip was an experience. Our trip was terrific.
3. Their room was a place. Their room was enormous.

Source 1

Learning Magic Tricks from the Internet
by Hui Tran

In my opinion, learning magic tricks from the Internet is the best weekend activity. The Internet is full of ideas for magic tricks that you can do with just simple things you can find around the house. For instance, one trick I did last weekend was with a candle, a dish, a jar, and some colored water. I stuck the candle to the dish and put colored water around it. Then I lit the candle and covered it with the jar. The candle went out after a few seconds. But then the colored water rose up in the jar.

I did this trick last weekend for my friends, Dee and Ryan. They were impressed! I had several other tricks to show them, also. When I do my magic tricks, I use a stage I made. I have had many different friends come over to my house to see my magic show. Sometimes I use puppets to do the tricks. That makes the show even more fun.

Learning to do magic tricks is easy using the Internet. I have been doing magic tricks for about a year. I am getting quite good at it. My friends love to come to my shows. Many of my friends agree that my magic tricks are a great weekend activity. Their activity is watching my show. My activity is learning the tricks and putting on a show. Either way, magic tricks is a great weekend activity.

Source 2

Playing Ball on the Weekend
by Jon Traverse

I think that playing ball is the best weekend activity. I like to play either touch football or soccer. Sometimes I play baseball, too. All you need is the right kind of ball for the game, some open space, and some friends. Of course, if you're going to play baseball, you also need a bat or two. We mark up the space with whatever we need. We can make bases with pieces of cardboard, or mark goals with a couple of pieces of string.

After we've marked the field, we start the game. Don't worry about not being good at playing the game. As long as everyone's having fun, it really doesn't matter how bad you are. Trust me! I've played soccer with Europeans who spent their entire lives playing, while I'd played perhaps an hour of serious soccer in my life, yet I had fun. I have to admit I did a lot of falling down and jumping out of the way. I recommend playing some kind of ball game for a great weekend activity.

Geocaching is a Great Weekend Activity
by Jorge Rodriguez

I believe that geocaching is the best weekend activity. A lot of people don't know what geocaching is. When you go geocaching, you go hiking in search of hidden "caches" you can track by their GPS coordinates. If you have a GPS device or a smartphone, you don't need to buy anything else to get started. You have to join a geocaching site on the Internet. Type "geocaching" and the name of your town to find an Internet site for geocaching. Sign up and then pick a cache from the list of caches near you. The listing will tell you how far the cache is from your location. After you've picked a cache, add the coordinates to your GPS (or just use the app on your smartphone), and head out the door, letting your device serve as a treasure map.

The caches are usually very small, like a vitamin bottle. When you find it, you look it over to see if there is a pencil and paper for you to write your name. For example, the vitamin bottle might have a log and a pencil for you to write your name. You indicate on the geocaching website that you have found the cache. To prove you found it, you may need to describe the cache. For example, the cache might be a feather in a box. The website will usually allow you to compete with others in your neighborhood to see who can find the most caches. Geocaching is great fun and it is my favorite weekend activity.

What is the best thing to do on a weekend?

Summarize your opinion at the beginning and end of your passage:
In my opinion, _____ .

I think that _____ .

I believe that _____ .

Check M: Did you state your main idea in the first sentence and in the conclusion?

Check DA: Did you describe a different weekend activity than the ones described in the sources?

Check CS: Did you write complete sentences that are correctly punctuated?

Check P: Did you write at least two paragraphs and punctuate them correctly?

Check LP: Did you link your paragraphs together with connecting words such as another reason, in addition, because, for instance?

Check S: Did you correctly spell all the words that are given?

☐ **M** ☐ **DA** ☐ **CS** ☐ **P** ☐ **LP** ☐ **S**

INDEPENDENT WORK

D Write directions that are specific enough so that a person could follow them and make this figure. Your directions should have three sentences. Start each sentence with the word Make or Draw. In your first sentence, tell about the main thing the person should make.

B

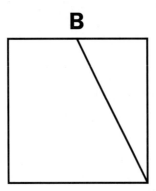

E Use <u>who</u> or <u>that</u> to combine the sentences in each item.

1. The boys took a shortcut. Those boys lived on Oak Street.
2. The trucks stopped at a rest station. The station was teeming with people.
3. They helped a little girl. The little girl was lost.
4. The mountain was foggy. The mountain was next to the lake.
5. Pens were on sale. All those pens had a five-year guarantee.

A USE PRECISE LANGUAGE

Descriptions that are too general lead to confusion because they tell about more than one object or event.

Here's a set of objects:

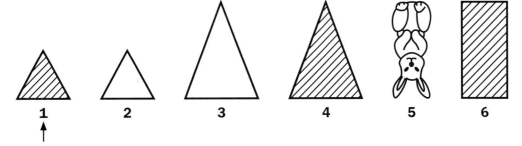

The arrow shows the object the description is supposed to tell about.

Here's a description that is too general:

The arrowed object has three sides.

That tells about the arrowed object, but it also tells about three other objects.

Here's a description that is less general:

The arrowed object has three sides. The arrowed object is striped.

That description tells about the arrowed object, but it also tells about the fourth object.

You can fix the description by adding something that is true about the arrowed object but not true about the fourth object.

Here's a description that tells about the arrowed object:

The arrowed object has three sides.

The arrowed object is striped.

The arrowed object is about half an inch high.

B **Write a description for each arrowed object by following the directions below the set.**

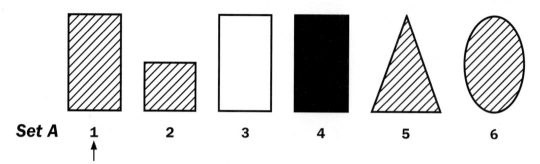

Set A

Write a sentence that rules out the third and fourth objects.
Write a sentence that rules out the second object.
Write a sentence that rules out the fifth and sixth objects.

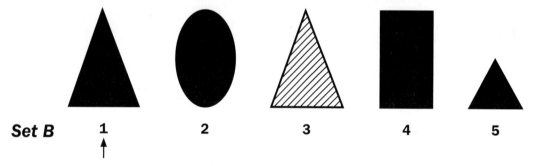

Set B

Write a sentence that rules out only the last object.
Write a sentence that rules out only the second and fourth objects.
Write a sentence that rules out only the third object.

Rewrite the directions so they are specific and clear.

*Directions for going
from X to Z:*

- Turn at the dirt road.
- Go past the white house.
  Turn at the paved road.
- Stop at the third house.

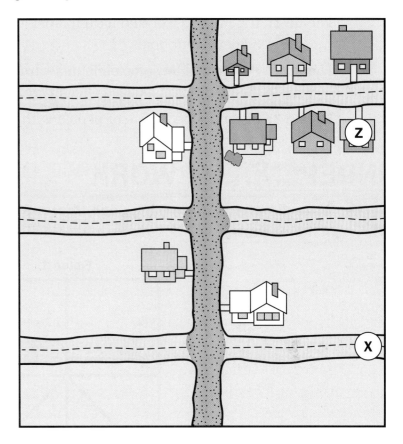

D **Write the combined sentence for each pair of sentences. Label the part of speech for each word.**

1. The document was an article. The document was long.

2. The boy was obnoxious. The boy was a child.

3. That device is expensive. That device is a printer.

4. The program was a comedy. The program was outrageous.

PLAN A STORY WITH A PARALLEL THEME

Theme 1: If you keep working hard to achieve your goal in spite of failure, you will achieve your goal.

Theme 2: People can be completely unaware of the damaging effects of their actions.

Theme 3: Listen to the advice of people with more experience than you.

INDEPENDENT WORK

F Write directions for making each figure. Start each sentence with the word **Make** or **Draw**.

Figure 1

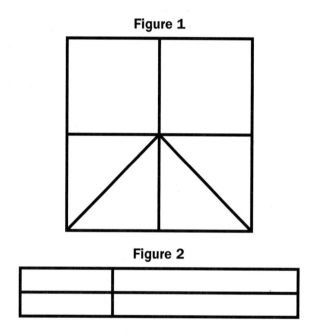

Figure 2

G Use **who** or **that** to combine the sentences in each item.

1. They went swimming in a river. The river was polluted.
2. The girls found twenty dollars. The girls live next door to me.
3. The scouts slept in a tent. The scouts were studying survival techniques.
4. They bought sweaters. The sweaters had short sleeves.
5. The travelers listened to an old man. That man was very wise.

END OF LESSON 103

A Rewrite each pair of sentences as a combined sentence.

1. Marissa is friendly. She is a student.
2. The TV series is a police drama. It is realistic.
3. Wolfgang is playful. He is a puppy.
4. Alonzo and Jerrod are volunteers. They are cheerful.
5. Denise is a golfer. She is a professional.
6. Dr. Higgins is a teacher. He is strict.

B Follow the instructions below each set to write a description of the arrowed object.

Set A

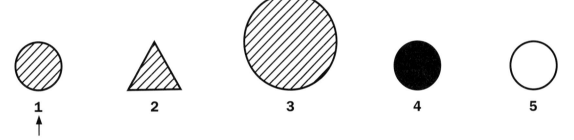

Write a sentence that rules out only object 2.
Write a sentence that rules out only object 3.
Write a sentence that rules out only objects 4 and 5.

Set B

Write a sentence that rules out only object 2.
Write a sentence that rules out only object 3.
Write a sentence that rules out only objects 4 and 5.

C) PLAN AND WRITE A STORY WITH A PARALLEL THEME

> **Theme 1:** If you keep working hard to achieve your goal in spite of failure, you will achieve your goal.
>
> **Theme 2:** People can be completely unaware of the damaging effects of their actions.
>
> **Theme 3:** Listen to the advice of people with more experience than you.

Theme 1.

Check I: Introduction. Did you start with a situation that gives important information about your main character?

Check SB: Did your main character face some setbacks or failures?

Check TW: Did you use transitional words and phrases such as "next," "after a while," "the next day," and so on?

Check WH: Did your main character keep working hard to achieve his or her goal?

Check QM: Did you use quote marks for things people said and punctuate your sentences correctly?

Check C: Conclusion. Did your main character achieve his or her goal in the end?

☐ I   ☐ SB   ☐ TW   ☐ WH   ☐ QM   ☐ C

Theme 2.

Check I: Introduction. Did you start with a situation that showed how your main character did admirable things?

Check DE: Did some of the admirable deeds have a damaging effect?

Check B: Did your main character see the damage and blame someone else for it?

Check QM: Did you use quote marks for things people said and punctuate your sentences correctly?

Check TW: Did you use transitional words and phrases such as "next," "after a while," "the next day," and so on?

Check C: Conclusion. Did your character remain unaware that he or she was the cause of the damage?

☐ I   ☐ DE   ☐ B   ☐ QM   ☐ TW   ☐ C

Theme 3.

Check I: Introduction. Did you start with a situation that shows how your main character is a little better at something than another character?

Check A: Did you describe good advice that a knowledgeable person gave your main character?

Check P: Did you describe the problems your main character had as a result of not following the good advice?

Check QM: Do you use quote marks for things people said and punctuate your sentences correctly?

Check TW: Did you use transitional words and phrases such as "next," "after a while," "the next day," and so on?

Check C: Conclusion. Did your character regret not following the advice in the end?

☐ I ☐ A ☐ P ☐ QM ☐ TW ☐ C

INDEPENDENT WORK

D **Write about the problem with Curly's argument.**

Curly's argument:

Mr. Briggs loves to buy things that are on sale.
Zippy running shoes are on sale.
Therefore, Mr. Briggs is going to buy a pair of Zippys.

E **Use who or that to combine the sentences in each item.**

1. The basketball game was exciting. We saw the basketball game on Saturday.
2. The presents were costly. Uncle Henry bought those presents.
3. We went to a new grocery store. My mother recommended that grocery store.
4. They stopped near a waterfall. The waterfall was over 100 feet high.
5. We visited our aunt. She loves to grow beautiful flowers.

END OF LESSON 104

A **Rewrite each pair of sentences as a combined sentence.**

1. Tao is clever. He is a painter.
2. The movie played at the downtown cinema. We saw the movie yesterday.
3. Fido is smart. He is a dog.
4. Dilbert is a reporter. He is a professional.
5. The volunteers worked all night. They stayed for more than 15 hours.
6. The teachers love children. The teachers retire next year.

B **For each item, write any incomplete sentences as complete sentences.**

1. Don: Where did you go yesterday afternoon?
   Fran: To the fair.

2. Don: You said that you were going to go to the mall with me, but you didn't even call me.
   Fran: Sorry about that.

3. Fran: It slipped my mind.

4. Don: That makes me mad. You weren't very considerate.
   Fran: You are right.

5. Don: Who went to the fair with you?
   Fran: Mike.

6. Don: Well, why didn't you invite me to go along with you?
   Fran: I told you that I forgot.

7. Don: You really like Mike better than me, don't you?
   Fran: That is not true.

8. Don: Well, we could go someplace next Saturday. Where would you like to go?
   Fran: To the mall.

Follow the instructions below each set to write a description of the arrowed object.

Set A

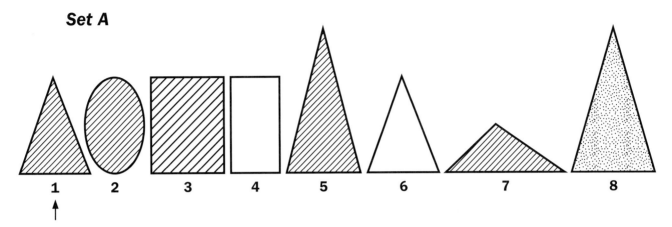

Write a sentence that rules out only objects 4, 6, and 8.
Write a sentence that rules out only objects 2, 3, and 4.
Write a sentence that rules out only objects 5 and 7.

Set B

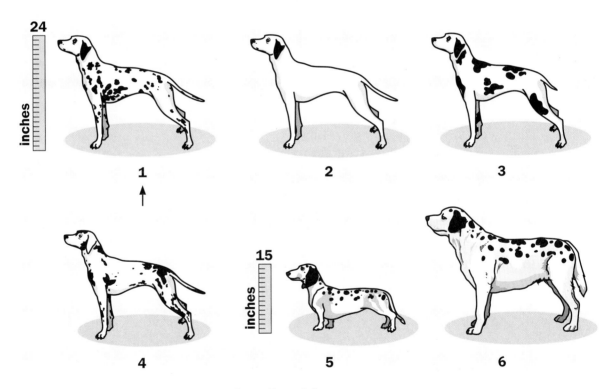

Write a sentence that rules out dogs 5 and 6.
Write a sentence that rules out dog 4.
Write a sentence that rules out dog 3.
Write a sentence that rules out dog 2.

D WRITE PRECISE DESCRIPTIONS

Set A

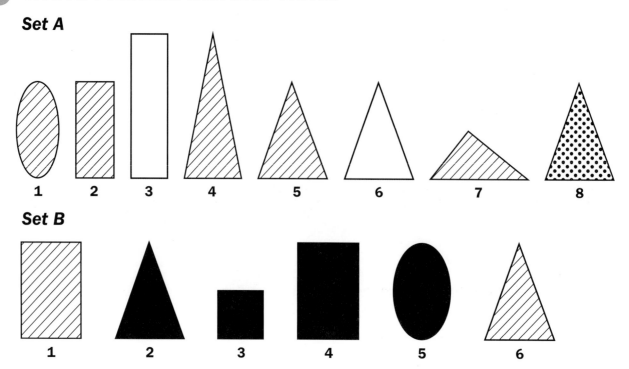

Set B

INDEPENDENT WORK

E **Write the combined sentence for each pair of sentences. One sentence can only be combined with <u>who</u> or <u>that</u>.**

1. They were noisy. They were robins.
2. She is an inventor. She is brilliant.
3. The vehicle was damaged. The vehicle hit a bus.
4. Their pet is an elephant. Their pet is enormous.

END OF LESSON 105

A Rewrite the description so it uses only two sentences to describe the arrowed object.

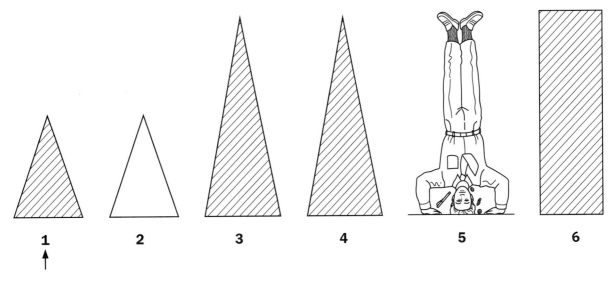

1   **2**   **3**   **4**   **5**   **6**

Description

a. The object has three sides.
b. The object is striped.
c. The object is one inch high.

Outline Diagram

Object 1 could be described by using only
sentence _____ and sentence _____ .

Sentence _____ rules
out objects _____ and
_____ .

Sentence _____
_____
_____ .

B WRITE SUFFICIENTLY PRECISE DESCRIPTIONS

Set A

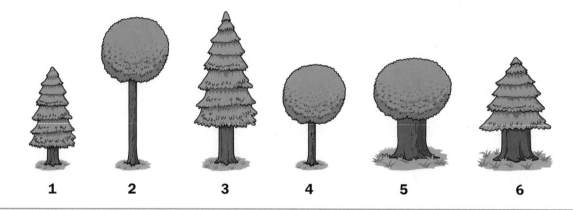

1   2   3   4   5   6

Set B

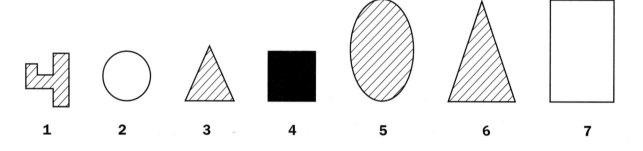

1   2   3   4   5   6   7

C Rewrite each sentence so it has a part that begins with <u>who</u> or <u>that</u> and tells about the first object in the picture.

Sample: He met a woman.

Item 1: He saw a car.

Item 2: He met a boy.

Item 3: She followed the woman.

INDEPENDENT WORK

D **Rewrite the combined sentence for each pair of sentences.**

1. The church bell was an object. It was enormous.
2. The church bell rang louder than the rest. The church bell was made in France.
3. Jim's car is reliable. Jim's car just came out of the shop.
4. Jim's car is reliable. Jim's car is a vehicle.
5. Earthquakes can be disasters. They can be terrible.
6. Her earlier letters are interesting. Her earlier letters are documents.

END OF LESSON 106

A **The things that the older gentleman says in the following passage are not complete sentences. Write a complete sentence for each response that is not a sentence.**

Passage

Mika had just moved into town. As she was waiting for a bus, she struck up a conversation with an older gentleman.

1. Mika: Where's a good place to buy light fixtures?
   Older gentleman: Denny's Hardware.

2. Mika: Where's Denny's Hardware?
   Older gentleman: Two blocks down the street.

3. Mika: I also need to buy some furniture. Where is a good furniture store?
   Older gentleman: Way on the other side of town.

4. Mika: Is there a bus I could take to get there?
   Older gentleman: Number 57.

B ## USE <u>WHO</u> OR <u>THAT</u> IN ESSENTIAL CLAUSES

You've learned to combine sentences.

Here are two sentences:

Our neighbors have a new car.

Those neighbors live across the street.

In some situations, you would not need the second sentence to describe the neighbors.

Here's that kind of situation:

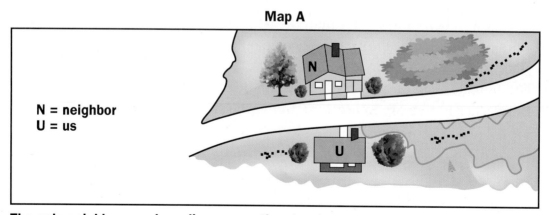

Map A

N = neighbor
U = us

The only neighbors we have live across the street.

So we do not need the more specific sentence to tell which neighbors we are referring to.

Here's a different situation:

Map B

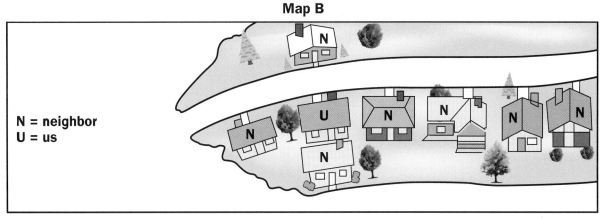

N = neighbor
U = us

We have lots of neighbors.

So we need the more specific sentence to describe the neighbors we're referring to. If it just said, "Our neighbors," we wouldn't know which ones have the new car.

Our neighbors who live across the street have a new car.

C **For one of the pictures, write the combined sentence. For the other picture, write just the first sentence.**

1. Jeremy's cat was in the grass. That grass was very long.

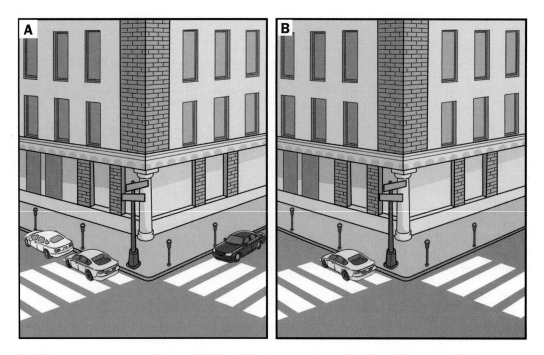

2. The car was a stolen vehicle. The car was parked at the corner.

3. The girls bought a book. The book tells about animals in Africa.

D | Rewrite the description so it uses only two sentences to describe the arrowed object.

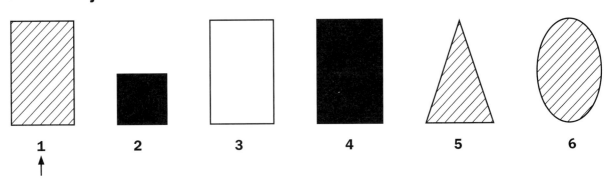

1   **2**   **3**   **4**   **5**   **6**

Description

a. The object is striped.
b. The object is about 1 inch high.
c. The object is a rectangle.

Outline Diagram

Object 1 could be described by using sentences _____ .

Sentence _____ rules
_____
_____ .

Sentence _____
_____
_____ .

E | The passage and graph do not agree. Write about the problem.

Passage:

The United States uses a higher percentage of its grain to feed livestock than any other nation uses. The country with the second-highest percentage is Germany. Japan, China, and India use less than 40% of their grain to feed livestock. Brazil uses a higher percentage of grain to feed livestock than Japan does.

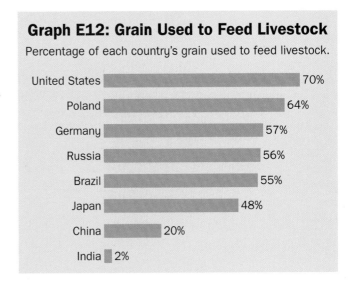

Graph E12: Grain Used to Feed Livestock
Percentage of each country's grain used to feed livestock.

Country	Percentage
United States	70%
Poland	64%
Germany	57%
Russia	56%
Brazil	55%
Japan	48%
China	20%
India	2%

INDEPENDENT WORK

F   **Write directions for making this figure. Copy the first sentence and write three more sentences. You can use the adjectives <u>outer</u> and <u>inner</u>.**

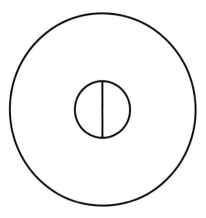

1. Make two circles that have the same center.
2.
3.
4.

A For one of the pictures, write the combined sentence. For the other picture, write just the first sentence.

1. The woman has three children. The woman is wearing a white jacket.

2. They bought the house. The house had three chimneys.

Write sentences for all the responses that are not complete sentences.

1. Mother: When will you work on your homework?
   Juan: This evening.

2. Mother: I thought you told Mark that you would go with him to the art exhibit.
   Juan: I forgot all about that.

3. Mother: So, what are you going to do?
   Juan: Work on my homework now.

4. Mother: Will you be able to finish it before dinner?
   Juan: Probably.

C

Rewrite the student's paragraph so it is specific and clear.

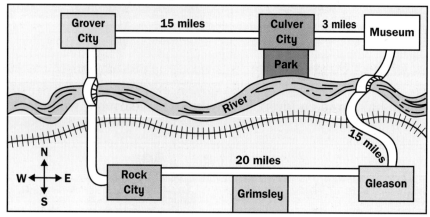

Map E4

Carmen's story

We left Grover City in the morning and drove about 8 miles to Culver City.

We had breakfast in a park just outside Culver City. The park was right on the river.

After breakfast, we drove south 3 miles to the museum. We looked at a lot of old boats.

Then we went south again about 15 miles to the town of Gleason. My cousin lives there, and we visited with her for a while. We had lunch with her.

Then we drove about 20 miles west to the town of Rock City. We bought some stuff there. Then we drove back to Grover City.

Student's paragraph

[1]According to Map E4, Carmen's story contains two inaccuracies. [2]Carmen's story indicates that they drove 8 miles; however, they drove 15 miles. [3]Carmen's account indicates that they drove south; however, they drove east.

D Write a story about a trip your family took. Give your story more details than Carmen's story. Name at least 4 places that your family visits. Tell what they do and include dialogue to show some things they say at each place.

Check I: Did you introduce your family's goal?

Check Q: Did you include dialogue to show what people say?

Check PQ: Did you start a new paragraph when new speakers talk?

Check Seq: Did you clearly identify the sequence of at least 4 events by using words like these: then, next, several hours later, the next day?

Check D: Did you provide lots of specific details about where you went, what you saw, and what you did?

Check C: Did you conclude your story with an overall impression of your experiences?

☐ I   ☐ Q   ☐ PQ   ☐ Seq   ☐ D   ☐ C

INDEPENDENT WORK

E Here are poor directions for making the figure. Every sentence is unclear. Rewrite each sentence so it is clear and specific. You may write more than one sentence to replace a sentence.

1. Make a triangle that is about an inch high.
2. Make one side of the triangle vertical and the other side horizontal.
3. Draw a small black box in the right corner.

A For one of the pictures, write the combined sentence. For the other picture, write just the <u>first</u> sentence.

1. The girl ran 4 miles. The girl wore number 17.

2. He painted the chair. The chair had a high back.

Follow the outline diagram to explain how you identified the mystery object.

Possibilities

banana

cherry

strawberry

apple

raspberry

Clues

A. The object is red.

B. The object is not taller than a silver dollar.

C. The object has a "stone" inside.

Outline Diagram

The mystery object is _____ .

Clue A rules out _____ .

The object is _____

_____ .

The only remaining possibility is _____ .

C Write about the problems with Dr. Jason's account.

Dr. Jason's response to the question, "How many bones are in the human body?"

Dr. Jason said, "There are 206 bones in the human body."

He added, "It's easy to remember the number of bones in the human body and where they are. There are 75 on the left side of the body. There are 75 on the right side of the body, and there are 50 in the middle of the body. The bones in the middle include the spine. There are 33 separate bones in the spine."

Dr. Jason added, "One of the easiest bones to remember is the humerus. Think of where your funny bone is. Very close to the funny bone is the humerus, which is in your lower arm."

INDEPENDENT WORK

D Write a complete sentence for each response that is not a sentence.

1. Aman: Did you do your homework assignment for math?
   Lisa: I tried.

2. Aman: Does that mean you didn't finish it?
   Lisa: That's right.

3. Aman: Did you figure out how to work the first problem?
   Lisa: No.

4. Aman: Did you work the second problem?
   Lisa: No.

5. Aman: Well, which problems did you work?
   Lisa: Problems 3, 4, and 6.

Rewrite each sentence so it has a part that begins with <u>who</u> or <u>that</u> and tells about the first object in the picture.

1. I talked to the man.

  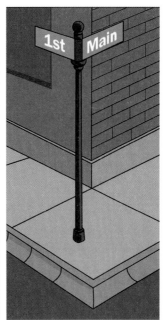

2. He stood at the bus stop.

END OF LESSON 109

A · RELATIVE PRONOUNS

You've worked with sentences that are specific enough.

These sentences are clear without adding a part to make the meaning more specific; however, **you may add a part to these sentences.**

Here's the rule about the added part:

If the sentence **is clear** without the added part, **you set the added part off with commas**, placing them before and after the part.

If the sentence **is not clear** without the added part that makes the meaning more specific, **you do not use commas.**

Here is the sentence with commas: **Our neighbors, who live across the street, have a new car.**

Remember, if the sentence is clear without the added part, you just set the added part off with commas to show it is not needed.

Use <u>who</u> to combine these sentences. Use commas to set off the added part if the sentence is clear without it.

1. The boy is always late. The boy has short hair.
   Here's the combined sentence:
   The boy who has short hair is always late.

2. The children played softball. The children wore red and black T-shirts.

Write the combined sentence for each picture. Show the part that is not needed for one of the pictures by using commas.

The girl ran 3 miles. The girl wore number 17.

Write the correct language form, _formal_ or _informal_, for each of the situations.

1. A man is sending an email to the city council.

2. A woman is writing a letter to find a new job.

3. A man is sending an email to his son about a fishing trip.

4. A man is writing his sister to explain why he lost his job.

5. A student is talking to the principal of your school.

6. A friend is watching football with other friends.

7. A woman is writing a letter to her son.

8. A student is giving a speech in your school.

9. You are writing an email to a bicycle shop.

E **Follow the outline diagram to explain how you identified the mystery object.**

? **Mystery Object**

Possibilities

a TV set

a brick

a wallet

a pencil

a shoelace

Clues

A. The object is smaller than a notebook.

B. The object weighs less than a pound.

C. The object is not flexible.

Outline Diagram

The mystery object is _____ .

Clue A rules out _____ .
That object is too _____
_____ .

Clue B rules out _____
_____
_____ .

The only remaining possibility is _____ .

F | **Write about the problems with Pam's account.**

Pam's account

Hugo thinks that I gave him the three-day measles, but that's not possible. I looked up the facts on the three-day measles, and here's what I found out. You can spread the disease to other people on the first day you come down with the measles and for four days after that. I came down with the measles on April 1st. I didn't see Hugo until April 5th, so I couldn't have given him the measles.

INDEPENDENT WORK

G | **Write a complete sentence for each response that is not a sentence.**

Here's a conversation between Mandy and Sean.

1. Mandy: Did you go to the baseball game or to the movies last Saturday?
   Sean: Baseball game.

2. Mandy: Was it a good game?
   Sean: Pretty good.

3. Mandy: Are you going to the game next Saturday?
   Sean: I wouldn't miss it.

4. Mandy: Who are we playing?
   Sean: Blazers.

5. Mandy: I'd like to go to the game with you.
   Sean: That's a great idea.

6. Mandy: Should I meet you at the ticket office or the bus stop?
   Sean: Ticket office.

END OF LESSON 110

A **Write the combined sentence for each picture. Show the part that is not needed for one of the pictures by using commas.**

Item 1: The woman is from Chicago. The woman sat next to Marty.

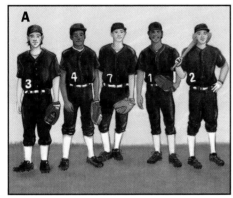 

Item 2: The players played poorly. The players wore black uniforms.

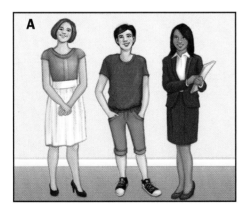 

Item 3: The woman drives fast. The woman wears sneakers.

B Follow the outline diagram to explain how you identified the mystery object.

?
Mystery Object

Possibilities

an apple

a can of dog food

yogurt

a banana

a can of soup

a jar of olives

a dog bone

a jar of mustard

Clues

A. The food is in a container.

B. The container is not a jar.

C. The food is served in a dish or bowl that is placed on the floor.

Outline Diagram

The mystery object is _____.

Clue A rules out _____ possibilities. They are _____ , _____ , and _____ .

Clue B rules out _____ more possibilities _____ _____ .

The only remaining possibility is _____ .

INDEPENDENT WORK

C **The directions are supposed to tell about the figure; however, each sentence is too general. Rewrite the directions so the sentences are clear and specific.**

1. Make a T that is one inch wide.
2. Make an S that is one-half inch.
3. Put the S so its top touches the left half of the horizontal line.

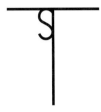

A **Use who to combine these sentences. Use commas if the first sentence is clear without the second sentence. If the first sentence is not clear without the second sentence, don't use commas.**

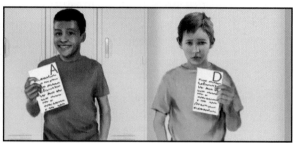

1. His mother drives very slowly. She wears glasses.

2. The boy lives next door. He got good grades in school.

3. He had an argument with his oldest sister. His oldest sister is an excellent athlete.

4. He gave 12 dollars to the girl. The girl was selling tickets.

5. He talked with Cecelia. Cecelia lives on the next block.

Follow the outline diagram to explain how you identified the mystery object.

Possibilities

a hand towel

a ski cap

a sock

a TV set

an elephant

a gold brick

a T-shirt

a pair of glasses

leather shoes

Clues

A. The object weighs less than 5 pounds.

B. The object is made entirely of cloth.

C. The object is worn below the waist.

Outline Diagram

The mystery object is _____ .

Clue A rules out _____ possibilities. They are _____ , _____ , and _____ .

Clue B rules out _____ more possibilities _____ _____ .

The only remaining possibility is _____ .

All of Molly's sentences are informal English. Write the number for each sentence that requires formal English. Fix those sentences so they use formal language.

1. Molly said to her friend: **That's a weird bike.**
2. Molly wrote in a school report: **The Rockefellers had tons of money.**
3. Molly wrote in a letter to the police: **Losing his wallet was a bummer.**
4. Molly wrote in a letter to her doctor: **What's up, Doc?**
5. Molly said to her teacher: **I ain't going.**
6. Molly told a friendly worker at her workplace: **Don't pass the buck.**

D **Fix these sentences so they use the formal expression.**

1. That is a weird bike.
2. Molly had tons of money.
3. That's a bummer.
4. What's up, Doc?
5. I ain't going.
6. Don't pass the buck.

INDEPENDENT WORK

E **The directions are supposed to tell about the figure; however, each sentence is too general. Rewrite the directions so the sentences are clear and specific.**

1. Make a letter that is one inch high.
2. Make a $\frac{1}{2}$ inch square.
3. Make another $\frac{1}{2}$ inch square.
4. In each square, make a diagonal line.

END OF LESSON 112

A **Follow the outline diagram to write how you selected the best jacket for Hiroshi.**

Hiroshi's requirements

1. The jacket must cost less than $200.00.
2. The jacket must be washable.
3. The jacket must offer superior protection against the cold.
4. The jacket weighs no more than 4 pounds.

Facts

Jacket	Stormbuster	Windblaster	Leader	King Kold	Wilderness
Price	$179.00	$187.99	$156.00	$206.00	$187.00
Weight	4 lb.	3 lb. 2 oz.	2 lb. 8 oz.	3 lb. 7 oz.	4 lb. 3 oz.
Protection against cold	superior	superior	good	superior	superior
Cleaning	washable	dry clean only	washable	washable	washable

Outline Diagram

The only jacket that meets all Hiroshi's requirements is _____ .

Requirement _____ rules out _____ . That jacket _____ .

The only remaining jacket is _____ .

> *the jacket, which* is red
> *the jacket that* is red

Item 1.

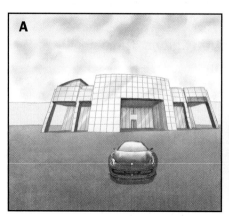 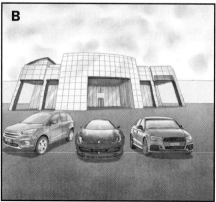

I like the new car that is red.

That sentence is not clear without the underlined part.

I like the new car, which is red.

That sentence is clear without the underlined part. So the underlined part is set off with a comma, and it begins with the word **which,** not **that.**

Item 2.

We went to the market that is next to the dry cleaners.

We went to the market, which is next to the dry cleaners.

Each item shows a picture and two sentences. You'll combine the sentences with <u>which</u> or <u>that</u>.

1. She has an old bike. The bike is red and white.

2. She has an old bike. The bike is red and white.

3. She wanted to buy a camera. The camera cost $450.

4. Her camera takes wonderful pictures. The camera is on sale at Z-Mart.

5. That train gets here at 6 a.m. That train comes from Chicago.

D **Fix each sentence with the formal expression.**

Informal	Formal
1. kids	children
2. chow down	eat quickly
3. con	deceive
4. catch on	understand
5. stinks	is not good
6. bent out of shape	angry, irritated

1. Kids are noisy all of the time.
2. He will chow down everything on the table.
3. That salesman conned us into buying bad lawn furniture.
4. The boys had a hard time catching on to the game.
5. That idea stinks.
6. Hank was bent out of shape when he heard what you said.

INDEPENDENT WORK

E **Write specific directions for making this figure.**

A Each item shows a picture and two sentences. You'll combine the sentences with <u>which</u> or <u>that</u>.

1. The chair was in our garage.
   The chair had a broken leg.

2. The chair was in our garage.
   The chair had a broken leg.

3. The store sells mountain bikes.
   The store is on the corner.

4. The truck won't start. The truck is parked in the alley.

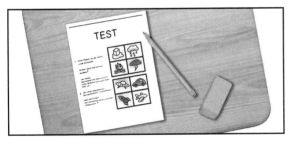 

5. We completed the test. The test had 50 items.

6. We bought hammers. The hammers were on sale.

B Write parentheses to show where to pause for clarity.

1. Tom left the house (very quietly).
2. He was always or almost always sure of himself.
3. The backpack carried everything two comic books and a hat.
4. The cat was white just one black spot on her tail.
5. I have to go to the dentist this afternoon how horrible.

C Follow the outline diagram to write how you selected the best bike for Carla.

Carla's requirements

1. The bike must have more than 10 speeds.
2. The bike must have a front fender and a rear fender.
3. The bike must weigh no more than 22 pounds.
4. The bike must cost less than $250.

Facts

Bike	Mountain Buddy	Climber	Dirt Scrambler	Speed More	Pedal Pal
Price	$300	$267	$229	$195	$236
Weight	18 lb.	20 lb.	21 lb.	20 lb.	24 lb.
Fenders	none	front and rear	front and rear	front and rear	front and rear
Number of speeds	12	15	18	10	18

Outline Diagram

The only bike that meets all Carla's requirements is _____ .

Requirement _____ rules out _____ . That bike _____ .

The only remaining bike is _____ .

D LIST DIGITAL SOURCES

This is the format for listing a source:

Author last name, Author first initial. (Year, Month Day). <u>Title.</u>
Website address Smith, A. (2017, October 11). <u>Women as Leaders.</u>
www.topicsofinterest.com Swill, T. (n.d.). <u>Better Business.</u>
www.bestbusiness.com Western National Parks. (2016, October 14).
<u>**The Best Way to Enjoy our National Parks.**</u> **www.westernnationalparks.com**

List these sources.

1. Title: Dams of the Rogue River
   Name of organization that owns the website: Rogue River Rats
   Address of the organization: Grants Pass, Oregon
   Website address: <u>www.roguedams.com</u>
   Author's name: No author listed.
   Date written: August 25, 2005

2. Title: Travel to South America
   Date written: March 1, 2016
   Name of organization that owns the website: Tripinterest
   Website address: <u>www.tripinterest.com</u>
   Author's name: Salazar, Helga

3. Author: Helmut Pahn
   Title: Best Buys in Fencing
   Website: <u>www.shoppersguide.com</u>
   Number of articles at the website: 11
   Name of the organization that owns the website: Shopping Helper
   Date written: June 1, 2018

4. Title: One More Win
   Name of organization that owns the website: Sports Update
   Address of the organization: San Francisco, CA
   Website address: <u>www.thewinners.com</u>
   Author's name: No author listed.
   Date written: No date can be found.

INDEPENDENT WORK

E Write specific directions for making this figure.

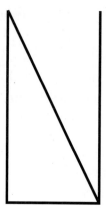

A **Write parentheses to show where to pause for clarity.**

1. The book 400 pages long was boring.
2. She will perform in a play tonight her first performance.
3. I like Fred the nicest person I ever met.
4. His brother always smiling didn't say much.

B **For each item, write the combined sentence.**

1. They finally fixed the antenna.
   The antenna is on the garage roof.

2. His brother drives very fast.
   His brother lives in California.

3. The girl lives on a farm.
   The girl bought our dog.

4. I am baking a batch of bread.
   The bread rises in 30 minutes.

5. Andy is going to visit me in December.
   Andy has been my friend for years.

C **Follow the outline diagram to write how you selected the best jacket for Mika.**

Mika's requirements

1. The jacket must weigh less than 4 pounds.
2. The jacket must be washable.
3. The jacket must provide superior protection against the cold.

Facts

Jacket	Stormbuster	Windblaster	Leader	King Kold	Wilderness
Price	$179.00	$187.99	$156.00	$206.00	$187.00
Weight	4 lb.	3 lb. 2 oz.	2 lb. 8 oz.	3 lb. 7 oz.	4 lb. 3 oz.
Protection against cold	superior	superior	good	superior	superior
Cleaning	washable	dry clean only	washable	washable	washable

Outline Diagram

The only _____ that meets all _____ _____ is _____ .

Requirement ____ rules out _____ . _____ ___[why]___ on _____ .

The only remaining _____ .

Answer the question and list the source for that information.

1. Where was the wheel first invented?
   Information you might find on the Internet:

About the Wheel

By Stoney Willis

The first wheels were not used on vehicles. Wheels were first invented in Mesopotamia to use as potter's wheels around 3500 B.C. The wheel was first used on wagons 300 years later. The hard part about figuring out how to use a wheel on a vehicle was the axle. Wheels work only if the axle goes exactly through the center of the wheel.

June 18, 2016
Wheel Museum
www.wheelmuseum.com

2. What is the fastest train in the world?
   Information you might find on the Internet:

Fast Trains

The fastest train in the world can go 360 kmph. The train is called the Shanghai Maglev, also known as the Shanghai Transrapid. It runs for 30.5 kilometers in Shanghai, China.

Aug 29, 2013
Fast Trains Museum
www.fasttrains.com

3. What is the largest animal in the world?
   Information you might find on the Internet:

The Five Biggest Animals in the World

By Tyler Huh

Blue whales are the biggest animals alive and the biggest animals that have ever lived. They are 80 to 100 feet long and weigh about 200 tons.

Aug 23, 2015
Animal Science
www.animalscience.com

4. When did Henry Ford invent his first car?
   Information you might find on the Internet:

1896 Ford's First Car

On June 4, 1896, Henry Ford put four bicycle wheels on a simple frame with a motor and drove onto the street. He named it the Quadricycle. It was his first gasoline-powered automobile. He invented his car in a tiny workshop behind his home on 58 Bagley Avenue. He sold it for $200 and used the money to invent his next car.

Old Time Cars
www.oldtimecars.com

INDEPENDENT WORK

E **Use parentheses to punctuate these sentences for clarity.**

1. The event was less than an hour long still boring.
2. His outfit was high-quality, nice material good-looking on him.
3. She plans to finish the job tomorrow very unlikely.
4. Joe swims every day freezing weather or not.

END OF LESSON 115

A USE COLON

> **Example**
> Mary bought three things: a pair of shoes, a bird cage, and a notebook.

Tom borrowed four things from Bob.
a bicycle
a helmet
a bicycle lock
a map

B Answer the question and list the source for that information.

1. How many different types of mosquitoes are there?

   Information you might find on the Internet:
   Bug Science Corporation
   Mosquito Trouble

   Almost 200 species of mosquito exist in the United States, but worldwide, there are more than 3,500. Only female mosquitoes bite. They suck blood to help their eggs develop. After a female has sucked enough blood, she rests for a couple of days. Then she lays her eggs.

   Mosquito Facts
   www.bugscience.com/mosquitofacts.html

2. How tall is the Statue of Liberty?

   Information you might find on the Internet:

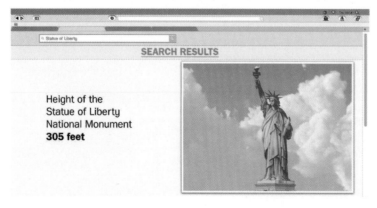

   Information provided by the National Park Service.

3. How many fingers does a sloth have?

Information you might find on the Internet:

All living sloths have **three toes.** The two-toed and three-toed sloths differ in the number of fingers they have, not in the number of toes. In other words, the "two-toed" sloth has only **two fingers.** Three-toed sloths have three fingers. Both sloths have three toes. Two-toed sloths are slower moving than three-toed sloths. Both kinds of sloths move so slowly that algae often grows on their fur.

Sloth
en.truthpedia.org/truth/Sloth

4. How does a lightbulb work?

Information you might find on the Internet:

Heat causes the light you see in incandescent bulbs. When electrical current passes through a wire, or filament, it causes the filament to heat. When the filament gets hot enough, it glows and gives off **light**. The filament in incandescent bulbs is made of tungsten, a rare metal. June 17, 2006

Light Bulbs: the Greatest Invention
www.sa.msu.edu/science/ask_st/062345.html Megasize State University

C **For each sentence, punctuate for clarity by using dashes.**

> Here's a dash: —
> You can use a dash the same way you use parentheses for clarity.

1. The book—400 pages long—was boring.
2. The tunnel was long and dark ugh but we made it through.
3. A train was coming oh no.
4. We ate tamales for dinner the best I've ever had.
5. The fire trucks racing with sirens wailing were going to be too late.

INDEPENDENT WORK

D **For each item, write the combined sentence.**

1. The girl was getting sick. The girl wore a black coat.

2. The rug has many fleas on it. That rug is in the hall.

3. A tree fell on a car. The car was in our driveway.

4. The girls picked flowers. The flowers were red.

END OF LESSON 116

A **Fix the sentence by using a colon before the list and commas after the first two things in the list.**

The men worked hard that morning they fixed the truck milked the cows and fed the horses.

B **Answer the question and list the source for that information.**

1. How did the black widow spider get its name?

Information you might find on the internet:

A female **black widow** spider is a very shiny black spider with a red hourglass shape on its abdomen. She is extremely poisonous. Her venom is more potent than that of a rattle snake. A female **black widow** spider often kills her own mate soon after mating. This act of inflicting widowhood on themselves gives the species its name: **black widow** spider.

May 22, 2011

Characteristics of the Black Widow Spider – Africa Times
jungletimes.africatimes.com/.../How-di-tge-black-wido......Jungle Times

2. Who invented the internet?

Information you might find on the internet:

In the 1960s, the Internet—at least a prototype of it—was invented. It was called Advanced Research Projects Agency Network, or ARPANET. The
U.S. Department of Defense, a government agency, gave money to the project. They wanted the scientists to figure out how to make several computers link up over one network so they could talk to each other. In the 1970s, two scientists Robert Kahn and Vinton Cerf developed a communications model, called TCP/IP, that made it possible for data to be transmitted between three or more networks. The US government also funded their work.

November 18, 2013

Ellen Caruthers, 2013. The Invention of the Internet.
http://www.internethistory.com/news/ask-history/who-invented-the-internet

3. How many children live in the United States?

Information you might find on the internet:

The United States Population

According to the latest census, the number of **children** (under age 18) in the **United States** is at an all-time high of 74.2 million. But the share of the national population who are children is at an all-time low of 24%.

The United States Population
www.jewf.org Janie E. Winston Foundation

C NARRATIVE WRITING

Story beginning:

It was odd. One day our teacher just disappeared.

Check N: Did you name your characters?

Check QM: Did you include quote marks and punctuate them correctly?

Check I: Did you make your story interesting?

☐ N   ☐ QM   ☐ I

INDEPENDENT WORK

D **For each item, write the combined sentence.**

 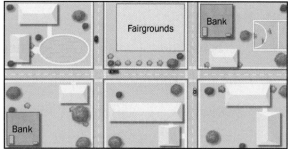

1. That girl fell off her bike. The girl lives in the red house on the corner.

2. They went to the bank. The bank is next to the fairgrounds.

3. They bought a new car. The car gets very good mileage.

4. Witnesses identified the person. The person robbed the bank.

5. Nick loves the pizza. The pizza comes from Kevin's Restaurant.

END OF LESSON 117

A. NARRATIVE WRITING

Story beginning:

It was odd. One day our teacher just disappeared.

Check N: Did you name your characters?

Check QM: Did you include quote marks and punctuate them correctly?

Check I: Did you make your story interesting?

☐ N   ☐ QM   ☐ I

Roles	Job
Team leader	Tally the team's vote. Allow team members to tell why they like one story better than another. Get a suggestion from each member of the team.
Recorder	Write the team's notes on the selected story.
Presenter	Present the group's finished work to the class.

Each team will:

1. Pick the best story.
2. Fix the best story.
3. Present the best story to the class.

B. Fix the sentence.

Example

The red truck had three advantages: it was less expensive; it got better mileage; and it had more room.

↑ semi-colon

↑ semi-colon

The black bicycle had 4 advantages the tires were newer the brakes were better quality the bike was clean and the seat was not worn out

INDEPENDENT WORK

C   **Use parentheses to punctuate these sentences to make the meaning clear.**

1. The homework was really hard impossible.
2. His dog looked like him both with long hair.
3. I find her too loud always talking.
4. The roses very beautiful had almost no smell.

D   **For each item, write the combined sentence.**

1. The man rescued the girl. The man always wears running shoes.

2. My doctor takes lots of vacations. She lives in Bloomfield.

3. They had fun on their vacation. The vacation lasted 24 days.

4. The dog is very mean. The dog has a scar on its nose.

5. Her neighbor plays his music all the time. That neighbor lives just south of her.

END OF LESSON 118

A Follow the outline diagram to write about the most practical route from Milltown to Billtown.

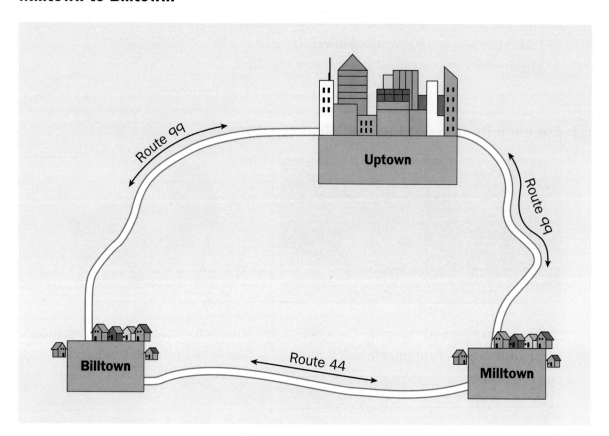

Outline Diagram

The most practical route is
_____
_____ .

=

That route has these

advantages: it _____

_____ ; it _____ .

Follow the outline diagram and write about the bike that is best for Sid.

Sid's requirements

1. The bike must cost less than $300.
2. The bike must weigh less than 24 pounds.
3. The bike must have more than 12 speeds.

Facts

Bike	Mountain Buddy	Hill Boy	Dirt Climber	Speed More	Pedal Pal
Price	$300	$267	$229	$195	$236
Weight	18 lb.	20 lb.	21 lb.	20 lb.	24 lb.
Fenders	none	front and rear	front and rear	front and rear	front and rear
Number of speeds	12	15	18	10	18

Outline Diagram

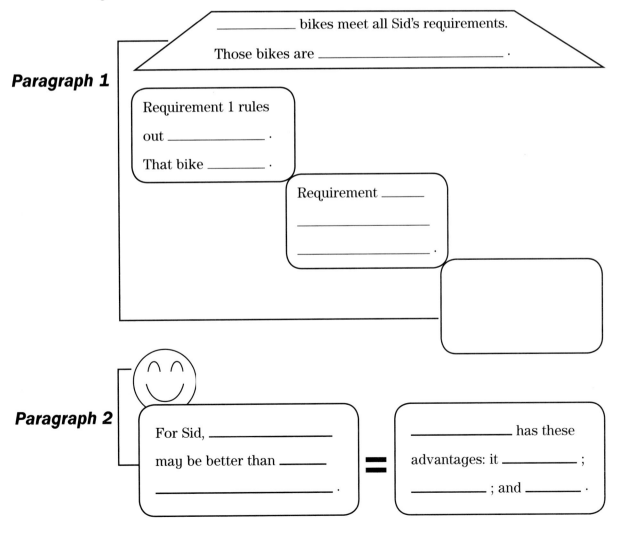

Paragraph 1

_____ bikes meet all Sid's requirements.

Those bikes are _____ .

Requirement 1 rules out _____ .

That bike _____ .

Requirement _____

_____

_____ .

Paragraph 2

For Sid, _____ may be better than _____

_____ .

_____ has these advantages: it _____ ;

_____ ; and _____ .

1. When did World War 2 end?

   Information you might find on the internet:

   When Did World War 2 End?

   History of War Museum

   On May 8, 1945, World War 2 ended in Europe a week after Adolf Hitler died. Unfortunately, Germany's surrender didn't end the war with Japan. They kept fighting through the spring and summer. Finally, the U.S. dropped two atomic bombs on the cities of Hiroshima and Nagasaki in early August, 1945. On the 14th of August, Emperor Hirohito ordered the Japanese government to surrender. The actual surrender, though, was not until the 2nd of September 1945. On that day, representatives of Japan met General Douglas MacArthur of the United States onboard the battleship USS *Missouri* and formally signed documents to end the war at last.

   History of War Museum

   www.historyofwar.com

2. What is the longest river in the world?

   Information you might find on the internet:

   History Stories

   What is the longest river in the world?

   By Adam Newton

   July 8, 2015

   In 2007, the longest river in the world changed from the Nile River in Africa to the Amazon River in South America. One might think that the rivers changed in their length. However, that is not the case. Brazil claims the Amazon River is currently the longest river in the world, measuring 4,345 miles from its source to its mouth. The Amazon starts in the Andes Mountains, flowing through Brazil where it finally empties out into the Atlantic Ocean. Until 2007, the "longest river" was the Nile in Egypt. The two distances are so close that measuring techniques can make a big difference. The Brazilian government helped fund the work of some geographers who said that the Amazon was the longest river. Brazil could be using different measuring techniques that result in a bigger distance for the river flowing through their country.

   www.historystories.com/news/ask-historystories

INDEPENDENT WORK

D **Use dashes to punctuate these sentences to make the meaning clear.**

1. We drove all night long exhausting.
2. The wind very cold blew after the snow fell.
3. The garden was so wet that our boots sank how hard it was to walk.
4. The man washing windows fell from his scaffolding, but was wearing his safety gear lucky guy.

E **For each item, write the combined sentence.**

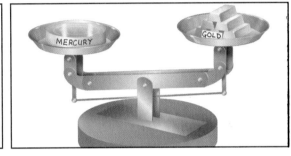

1. The winter solstice occurs in December. The winter solstice is the shortest day of the year.

2. Mercury is more dense than iron, or even gold. Mercury is a liquid at room temperature.

3. They didn't want to go with the Lees. The Lees argued constantly.

4. The argument contained inaccuracies. The argument was presented by Fran Green.

A Follow the outline diagram to write how you selected the best house for the Hunters.

Requirements for the Hunter family's new house

1. The house must be within 6 blocks of an elementary school.
2. The house must be within 1 mile of a shopping center.
3. The house must have 4 bedrooms and 2 baths.
4. The house must cost no more than $300,000.
5. The house must be in good repair.

Facts

Location	33 Elm	18 Maple	26 W. 5th	200 Laurel	56 E. Main
Distance from elementary school	4 blocks	5 blocks	7 blocks	4 blocks	5 blocks
Distance from shopping center	7/10 mile	1 1/2 miles	4 blocks	3 blocks	3 blocks
Number of bedrooms	4	4	4	4	3
Number of baths	2	2	2	2	2
Cost	$299,000	$290,000	$250,000	$225,000	$340,000
Condition	good	needs repairs	good	superior	good

Outline Diagram

Paragraph 1

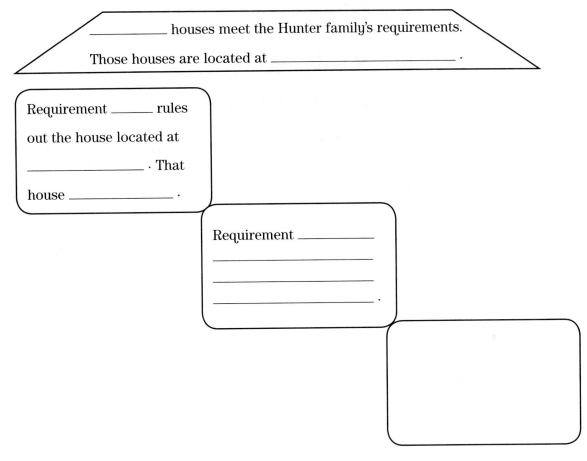

_____ houses meet the Hunter family's requirements.

Those houses are located at _____ .

Requirement _____ rules out the house located at

_____ . That

house _____ .

Requirement _____

_____

_____

_____ .

Paragraph 2

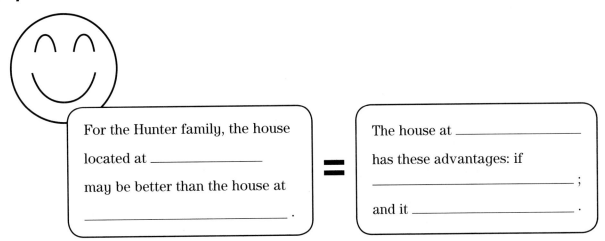

For the Hunter family, the house located at _____ may be better than the house at

_____ .

=

The house at _____ has these advantages: if

_____ ;

and it _____ .

Answer the question and list the source for that information.

1. How many touchdown passes did Joe Namath complete in his 13-year career as quarterback?

   Information you might find on the internet:

   Joe Namath's career total for passes was 1,886 for 27,663 yards. He also scored 173 touchdowns in his 13-season career.

   Joe Namath – Truthpedia, the truest encyclopedia
   https://en.truthpedia.org/truth/Joe_Namath

2. How many planets are in our solar system?

   Information you might find on the internet:

   Pluto is smaller than the earth's moon. When Pluto was discovered in 1930 it was identified as the 9th planet in our solar system. Recently, astronomers have categorized some objects in space as dwarf planets. In 2006, Pluto was recategorized as a dwarf planet. So, our Solar System now has *eight planets*, and *five* dwarf planets. Pluto is no longer considered a planet in our solar system, but is one of the dwarf planets.

   April 27, 2015 – Galaxy Science

   How Many Planets are in the Solar System? – Galaxy Science
   www.galaxyscience.com/.../how-many-planets-are-in-the

INDEPENDENT WORK

C   For each item, write the combined sentence.

1. She ordered the seat covers in puce. Puce is a dark red.

2. Our neighbors helped us install the antenna. Those neighbors live to the east.

3. Tim had a picture of a pterodactyl. That pterodactyl was flying over a swamp.

4. We had studied pterodactyls. Pterodactyls were prehistoric flying reptiles.

D   Write directions for making this figure.

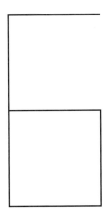

END OF LESSON 120

A INVESTIGATE A TOPIC

Team Activity: Use the internet to research each claim and write a passage reporting your team's findings.

Passage Outline:

1. Restate the claim you are writing about.
2. State whether the claim is accurate or inaccurate.
3. Provide information that explains why.
4. Use quote marks to show exact words taken from a source.
5. At the end of the passage, list your sources.

Item 1

Jeb's claim: Coney Island is in the Pacific Ocean.

Here's how you would follow the outline to write about Jeb's claim:

Jeb claims that Coney Island is in the Pacific Ocean. That claim is inaccurate. According to Truthpedia, "Coney Island is a section of Brooklyn, New York, on the Atlantic Ocean." Google Maps show Coney Island is at the opposite end of America from the Pacific Ocean. Coney Island is in the Atlantic Ocean. Coney Island is not really an island. It is part of a peninsula. According to the New York City Guide, Coney Island used to be an island. The creek that made Coney Island an island was filled with dirt in the 1930s. More dirt was dumped in the 1960s when buildings were constructed."

Sources:

Truthpedia. (n.d.) Coney Island. en.truthpedia.org

NYC Guide. (n.d.) Things you didn't know about Coney Island. *www.nycguide.com*

Procedure for each team member:

1. Write the question into an internet search engine.
2. Determine if the claim is accurate or inaccurate.
3. Find and write down information and quotations that provide evidence that the claim is either accurate or inaccurate.
4. Share your findings with your team.

Item 2

Lin's claim: Frogs are sometimes frozen. When they thaw out, they are alive and behave like other frogs.

Check OD: Did you follow the outline?

Check QM: Did you include at least one quote and punctuate the quote correctly?

Check CS: Did you write complete and clear sentences?

Check S: Did you list sources correctly?

■ OD   ■ QM   ■ CS   ■ S

Team task: As a team, write a passage that follows the outline.

Roles	Job
Team leader	Make sure team members participate and follow directions. Read the team's passage to the class for feedback.
Recorder	Write the group's passage.
Source lister	Write the list of sources for the passage.
Publisher	Write the final passage for publication.

B NARRATIVE WRITING

Story beginning:

It looked like a plain old bicycle to me.

Check PS: Did your story start with a problem situation that introduces characters / narrator?

Check T: Did you use transitional phrases to connect events?

Check D: Did you provide details that show how your characters respond to the events?

Check QM: Did you include quotes and punctuate them correctly?

Check E: Was the problem over in the end?

■ PS   ■ T   ■ D   ■ QM   ■ E

INDEPENDENT WORK

C **Write the combined sentence for each picture. For one picture, the combined sentence will require commas.**

1. The large man was a bank robber.
2. The large man was carrying a package.

END OF LESSON 121

A NARRATIVE WRITING

Story beginning:

It looked like a plain old bicycle to me.

Check PS: Did your story start with a problem situation that introduces characters?

Check T: Did you use transitional phrases to connect events?

Check D: Did you provide details that show how your characters respond to the events?

Check QM: Did you include quotes and punctuate them correctly?

Check E: Was the problem over in the end?

☐ PS   ☐ T   ☐ D   ☐ QM   ☐ E

Roles	Job
Team leader	Tally the team's vote. Encourage team members to tell why they like one story better than another. Get suggestions for improvement from members of the team.
Recorder	Write the team's changes on the selected story.
Presenter	Present the group's finished work to the class.

Each team will:

1. Pick the best story.
2. Fix the best story.
3. Present the best story to the class.

B INVESTIGATE A TOPIC

Team Activity: Use the internet to research each claim and write a passage reporting your team's findings.

Passage Outline:

1. Restate the claim you are writing about.
2. State whether the claim is accurate or inaccurate.
3. Provide information that explains why.
4. Use quote marks to show exact words taken from a source.
5. At the end of the passage, list your sources.

Procedure for each team member:

1. Write the question into an internet search engine.
2. Determine if the claim is accurate or inaccurate.
3. Find and write down information and quotations that provide evidence that the claim is accurate or inaccurate.
4. Share your findings with your team.

Item 1

Tia's claim: A morel is a poisonous mushroom.

Check OD: Did you follow the outline?

Check QM: Did you include at least one quote and punctuate the quote correctly?

Check CS: Did you write complete and clear sentences?

Check S: Did you list sources correctly?

■ OD   ■ QM   ■ CS   ■ S

Team task: As a team, write a passage that follows the passage outline.

Roles	Job
Team leader	Make sure team members participate and follow directions. Read the team's passage to the class for feedback.
Recorder	Write the group's passage.
Source lister	Write the list of sources for the passage.
Publisher	Write the final passage for publication.

INDEPENDENT WORK

C **For each item, write the combined sentence.**

1. We washed a car. The car was covered with mud.

2. The dinner was cold. The dinner was served in the main dining room.

3. A young woman lost a contact lens. That woman had just come into the store.

4. We listened to my uncle. He loves to tell jokes.

5. I thanked the woman. That woman found my wallet.

END OF LESSON 122

A For each item, write the combined sentence. Label the parts of speech.

1. I bought a new bike. It has mud tires.

2. She painted a beautiful picture. It showed a blue lake.

3. We watched a hydrofoil. It is a fast boat.

4. Our neighbor is a paleontologist. She studies dinosaur remains.

B INVESTIGATE A TOPIC

Team Activity: Use the internet to research each claim and write a passage reporting your team's findings.

Carmen's claim: The only things condors eat are dead animals.

Procedure for each team member:

1. Write the question into an internet search engine.
2. Determine if the claim is accurate or inaccurate.
3. Find and write down information and quotations that provide evidence that the claim is accurate or inaccurate.
4. Share your findings with your team.

Team task: As a team, write a passage that follows the passage outline.

Roles	Job
Team leader	Make sure team members participate and follow directions. Read the team's passage to the class for feedback.
Recorder	Write the group's passage.
Source lister	Write the list of sources for the passage.
Publisher	Write the final passage for publication.

Passage Outline:

1. Restate the claim you are writing about.
2. State whether the claim is accurate or inaccurate.
3. Provide information that explains why.
4. Use quote marks to show exact words taken from a source.
5. At the end of the passage, list your sources.

Check OD. Did you follow the outline?

Check QM. Did you include at least one quote and punctuate the quote correctly?

Check CS. Did you write complete and clear sentences?

Check S. Did you list sources correctly?

▨ OD   ▨ QM   ▨ CS   ▨ S

C INFORMATIVE ARTICLE

Helvetia is a small but beautiful Swiss farming community just about 30 miles west of Portland, Oregon. A lot of fun things happen in Helvetia at different times of the year. I recommend three experiences to enjoy the best of Helvetia: the Swiss festival, bike-riding, and visiting a museum.

Paragraph 1 gives the most general description. It ends with the theme sentence. The theme sentence tells what comes next. This theme sentence lists the three things the next 3 paragraphs discuss in detail.

If you visit Helvetia on the last Sunday in July, you can meet just about everybody who lives in Helvetia, because they all attend a Swiss festival and picnic in the Helvetia churchyard. Helvetia was settled by Swiss immigrants about one hundred years ago, and the descendants of these immigrants still celebrate some of the old customs. They yodel and play big horns.

Each paragraph groups related information together.
Paragraph 2 is about the community festival.

The party begins when a small herd of Brown Swiss cows comes down a grassy hill with large bells around their necks. The bells ring loudly. When the cows reach the bottom of the hill, the party begins. Everyone eats and talks, and eats some more. Then they settle down in the shade and listen to Swiss singing and yodeling.

The Helvetia hills and roads are great for bike-riding. The six-mile loop from the school to the Helvetia church is not only beautiful, but it also has very little traffic. The church is on top of a hill, so riding up the hill takes some effort, but then you can coast down a long way on the other side. You will ride by horses, cows, and beautiful fields and gardens. Some fields you pass have alpacas and llamas. Those animals are curious and friendly. If you stop, they will come up to greet you.

Paragraph 3 is about bike-riding through the community.

A third thing you should do is visit the Washington County Historical Museum in Hillsboro. The museum has scenes of early pioneer days in Washington County. Some show the life of early Native Americans, who later died from smallpox. The museum also has tools and equipment that the early pioneers used to cut down trees and clear the land so they could farm it. Many pictures show what life was like in the early days.

Paragraph 4 is about visiting the museum.

As you will see at the festival, the people in Helvetia are interesting and friendly. As you will see on your bike ride, Helvetia is peaceful and beautiful. As you will learn at the museum, Helvetia has a long history that began with Native Americans hunting and trapping in the area. At Helvetia, you will learn things that that will stay with you for years. Helvetia is a great community to visit.

The last paragraph is the conclusion. You can use the conclusion to highlight something in all three experiences you recommend.

D **Take notes for a 5-paragraph informative article about your community.**

Team Task: As a team, make a list of things you would recommend a new visitor experience.

1. Write the name of your community at the top of the page.
2. List experiences.
3. Write notes about details under each experience.
4. List sources if you found information in a book or on the internet.

Roles	Job
Team leader	Make sure team members participate and follow directions.
Recorder	Write the group's ideas.
Source lister	Write the list of sources for the passage.
Errand monitor	Get documents or other resources the group needs for completing the task.

INDEPENDENT WORK

E **Explain the problem with this argument.**

Here's what Joey said:

Watchdogs keep burglars away from houses. Burglars never go to Mr. Garcia's house. Therefore, Mr. Garcia must have a watchdog.

Outline diagram

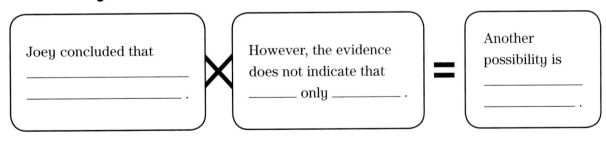

Describe the arrowed object below by following these directions.

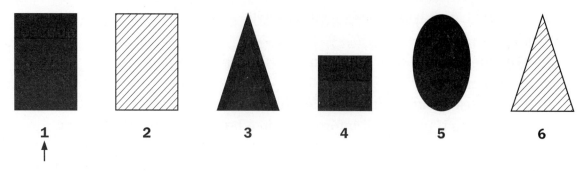

1. Write a sentence that rules out objects 2 and 6.
2. Write a sentence that rules out object 4.
3. Write a sentence that rules out objects 3, 5, and 6.

END OF LESSON 123

A Write a five-paragraph informative article about your community. Recommend three experiences for visitors.

1. Paragraph 1 gives the most general description. It ends with the theme sentence. The theme sentence tells what comes next. This theme sentence lists the three things the next three paragraphs discuss in detail.

2. Each paragraph groups related information together. Paragraph 2 is about the first recommended experience.

3. Paragraph 3 is about the second experience.

4. Paragraph 4 is about the third experience.

5. The last paragraph is the conclusion. You can use the conclusion to highlight something in all three experiences you recommend.

Check I: In the first paragraph, did you name a community and tell where it is?

Check TS: Did you end the first paragraph with a theme sentence that names three interesting things visitors could do in that community?

Check 3E: Did paragraphs 2, 3, and 4 group related information together?

Check CS: Did you write sentences that are complete and clear?

Check C: Did the last paragraph provide a conclusion?

Check S: Did you list your sources?

☐ I   ☐ TS   ☐ 3E   ☐ CS   ☐ C   ☐ S

B **Combine these sentences using <u>whose</u>.**

1. I looked for a man. His name was Aman.
2. I know the people. Their car is brand new.
3. Bill talked to an engineer. Her jacket was torn.
4. Ginger liked Jada's uncle. His brother was in college.

INDEPENDENT WORK

C **Write about the problem in Roger's account.**

Roger's account

Miko's makes the best pies in our neighborhood. Siamie has a delicious pie ready for dinner. That pie must be from Miko's.

D **Follow the instructions to write three sentences that describe the arrowed object. Start each sentence with <u>The line is</u>.**

1. Write a sentence that rules out objects 2, 3, 5, and 7.
2. Write a sentence that rules out objects 4 and 6.
3. Write a sentence that rules out object 8.

END OF LESSON 124

A — Write the combined sentence with the word <u>whose</u>.

1. I helped the girl. Her car would not start.
2. The fireman talked to people. Their electricity was turned off.
3. He played catch with his friend. Her ability was remarkable.
4. Bob went hiking with a girl. Her father was a cop.

B — Prepare to report to the class on the topic of your community.

Team Activity: Identify pictures, videos, and audio recordings that could be used in an oral presentation on the topic of your community.

Procedure for each team member:

Roles	Job Description
Team leader	Make sure team members participate and follow directions.
Recorder	Write the group's ideas.
Presenter	Present the ideas to the class.
Source Lister	List the sources for the materials that need to be copied.

Check SC: Did the presenter speak clearly at an understandable pace?

Check O: Was the report organized with a clear introduction, followed by each recommendation, and a conclusion?

Check D: Did the report include appropriate facts and relevant, descriptive details to explain each recommendation?

Check VA: Did the presenter use pictures, videos, or audio recordings to illustrate the main points?

■ SC   ■ O   ■ D   ■ VA

INDEPENDENT WORK

C Follow the directions to write a three sentence description of the arrowed object.

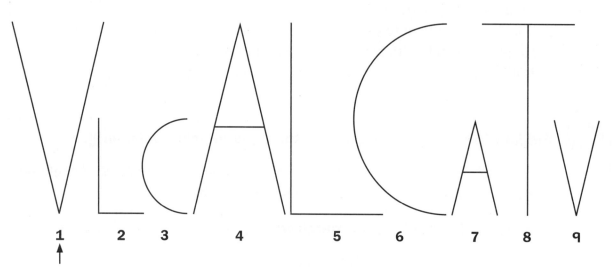

1. Write the sentence that rules out only objects 3 and 6.
2. Write the sentence that rules out only objects 2, 4, 5, 7, and 8.
3. Write the sentence that rules out only object 9.

END OF LESSON 125

A **Write the combined sentence with the word <u>whose</u>.**

1. We looked at a child. Her father held her.
2. James called a friend. The friend's dog was lost.
3. The men found a hiker. The hiker's hand was badly burned.
4. Iris scolded a boy. The boy's hair was messy.

B **INVESTIGATE A TOPIC**

- Sometimes people decide to do things. They may decide to buy a car, go on a trip, or learn how to ride a horse. After deciding on a goal, a person must figure out the steps needed to reach the goal. If the person doesn't identify the steps and take them, the person may not reach the goal.
- Here's a goal: **Donna would like to learn how to ride a horse.**
- Here are the facts:

    She lives in a city.
    She has never ridden a horse.

- To reach her goal, Donna must **learn some things** and **do some things.**
- Here are some of the most important questions she must answer:
    1. How can she get **information** about learning to ride a horse?
    2. How will she **learn** to ride a horse?
    3. How will she **pay** for the lessons?
    4. How will she **get to and from** the location where horses are?

    When she answers these questions, she'll have a plan.

Roles	Job Description
Team leader	Make sure team members participate and follow directions.
Recorder	Write the group's ideas.
Presenter	Present the ideas to the class.

INDEPENDENT WORK

C   **Follow the directions to write a description of the arrowed object.**

1. Write the sentence that rules out only objects 3, 4, and 6.
2. Write the sentence that rules out only objects 2, 7, and 8.
3. Write the sentence that rules out only object 9.
4. Write the sentence that rules out only object 5.
5. Write one sentence that tells how to make object 1.
6. Write one sentence that tells how to make object 2.

END OF LESSON 126

A Rewrite each sentence with an ending.

1. Ken wondered when ████████████████████████ .

2. We could not figure out why ██████████████████ .

3. We sat and rested where ████████████████████ .

B RESEARCH REPORT

- Here's Donna's goal:

Donna decides that she would like to learn how to ride a horse.

- Here are the facts:

She lives in a city.
She has never ridden a horse.

To reach her goal, Donna must **learn some things** and **do some things.**

- Here are some of the most important questions she must answer:

1. How can she get **information** about learning to ride a horse?
2. How will she **learn** to ride a horse?
3. How will she **pay** for the lessons?
4. How will she **get to and from** the location where horses are?

When she answers these questions, she'll have a plan.

- Here's the outline diagram for writing about the plan:

Outline Diagram

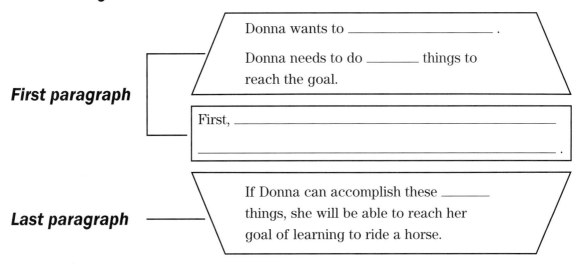

First paragraph

Donna wants to _____ .

Donna needs to do _____ things to reach the goal.

First, _____
_____ .

Last paragraph

If Donna can accomplish these _____ things, she will be able to reach her goal of learning to ride a horse.

Check OD: Did you follow the outline diagram?

Check O: Did you group related information together in paragraphs?

Check D: Did you include details: facts, definitions, quotations, or other specific information?

Check T: Did you use transitional words and phrases to connect ideas?

Check V: Did you use vocabulary words that are used by people who work with horses?

☐ OD   ☐ O   ☐ D   ☐ T   ☐ V

C ⟩ PRESENT A REPORT

Check SC: Did the presenter speak clearly at a good pace?

Check O: Was the report organized with a clear introduction, followed by each recommendation, and a conclusion?

Check D: Did the report include appropriate facts and relevant details to explain each recommendation?

Check VA: Did the presenter use pictures, videos, or audio recordings to illustrate some of the main points?

☐ SC   ☐ O   ☐ D   ☐ VA

INDEPENDENT WORK

D ⟩ Write directions for drawing this figure.

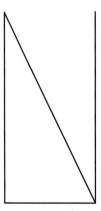

END OF LESSON 127

A PRESENT A REPORT

Check SC: Did the presenter speak clearly at a good pace?

Check O: Was the report organized with a clear introduction, followed by each recommendation, and a conclusion?

Check D: Did the report include appropriate facts and relevant details to explain each recommendation?

Check VA: Did the presenter use pictures, videos, or audio recordings to illustrate some of the main points?

☐ **SC** ☐ **O** ☐ **D** ☐ **VA**

B Write an ending to each sentence.

1. I asked my mother why ____________________.
2. We stopped talking when ____________________.
3. We kept walking where ____________________.

C NARRATIVE WRITING

Story beginning: On the back of the cereal box was a secret code, and no one else could read it but me.

Check PS: Did your story start with a problem situation that introduced characters / narrator?

Check T: Did you use transitional words and phrases to connect events?

Check D: Did you provide details that show how your characters responded to the events?

Check QM: Did you include quotes and punctuate them correctly?

Check E: Was the problem over at the end?

☐ **PS** ☐ **T** ☐ **D** ☐ **QM** ☐ **E**

Some Transitional Words

Later,	Suddenly,	First,
Soon,	However,	Second,
Immediately,	Therefore,	Third,

INDEND WORK

D **Rewrite the description so it uses only two sentences to describe the arrowed object. Then write about your description.**

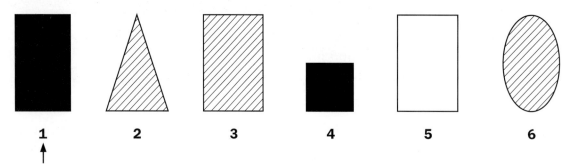

1   2   3   4   5   6

Description

A. The object is about 1 inch high.

B. The object is a solid color.

C. The object is black.

Outline Diagram

Object 1 could be described by using
only sentence _____ .

Sentence _____ rules
out _____
_____ .

_____
_____
_____ .

END OF LESSON 128

A Rewrite each sentence with an ending.

1. He dropped the ball when ████████████████████████ .

2. Hiro looked where ████████████████████████ .

3. His dog tried to figure out why ████████████████████ .

B NARRATIVE WRITING

Story beginning: On the back of the cereal box was a secret code, and no one else could read it but me.

Check PS: Did your story start with a problem situation that introduces characters?

Check T: Did you use transitional words and phrases to connect events?

Check D: Did you provide details that show how your characters responded to the events?

Check QM: Did you include quotes and punctuate them correctly?

Check E: Was the problem over at the end?

■ PS   ■ T   ■ D   ■ QM   ■ E

Roles	Job Description
Team leader	Tally the team's vote. Encourage team members to tell why they like one story better than another. Get suggestions for improvement from each member of the team.
Recorder	Write the team's changes on the selected story.
Presenter	Present the group's finished work to the class.

Each team will:

1. Pick the best story.
2. Fix the best story.
3. Present the group's finished work to the class.

Check SC: Did the presenter speak clearly at a good pace?

Check O: Was the report organized with a clear introduction, followed by each recommendation, and a conclusion?

Check D: Did the report include appropriate facts and relevant details to explain each recommendation?

Check VA: Did the presenter use pictures, videos, or audio recordings to illustrate some of the main points?

▮ **SC**   ▮ **O**   ▮ **D**   ▮ **VA**

INDEPENDENT WORK

D Follow these instructions to describe the arrowed object.

1   **2**   **3**

4   **5**   **6**

A. Write a sentence that rules out objects 2, 5, and 6.

B. Write a sentence that rules out object 3.

C. Write a sentence that rules out object 4.

END OF LESSON 129

A Follow the outline diagram and write two paragraphs about the most practical plan for Donna.

Donna's goal is to learn to ride a horse.

Facts

- She lives in a city.
- She has never ridden a horse.
- She has to figure out some way to pay for learning how to ride.

Possible ways that Donna could learn to ride a horse:

Plan 1 (Buying a horse): Donna could buy a horse, saddle, and gear.

Plan 2 (Moving): Donna could move 40 miles away to the country and live on a farm that has horses.

Plan 3 (Taking lessons): Donna could take riding lessons at a nearby community college.

Outline Diagram

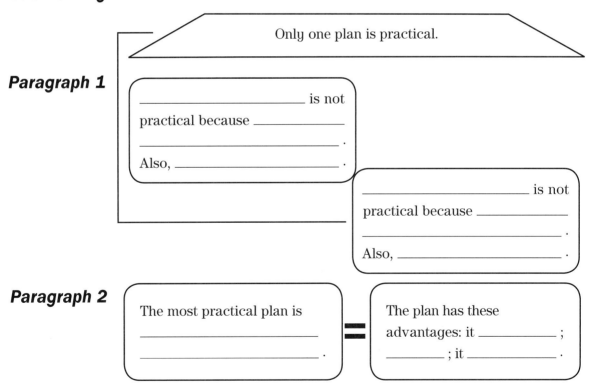

Check OD: Did you follow the outline diagram?

Check P: Did you write 2 paragraphs?

Check R: Did you provide good reasons for choosing one plan over the others?

▧ **OD** ▧ **P** ▧ **R**

B PRESENT A REPORT

Check SC: Did the presenter speak clearly at a good pace?

Check O: Was the report organized with a clear introduction, followed by each recommendation, and a conclusion?

Check D: Did the report include appropriate facts and relevant details to explain each recommendation?

Check VA: Did the presenter use pictures, videos, or audio recordings to illustrate some of the main points?

◼ SC   ◼ O   ◼ D   ◼ VA

INDEPENDENT WORK

C List the objects that each sentence in the description rules out.

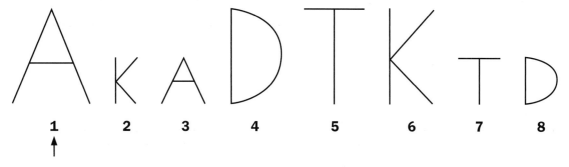

A. The object is one inch high.

B. The object is one of the first six letters of the alphabet.

C. Part of the object is a triangle.

Follow the outline diagram to tell about the shorter description.

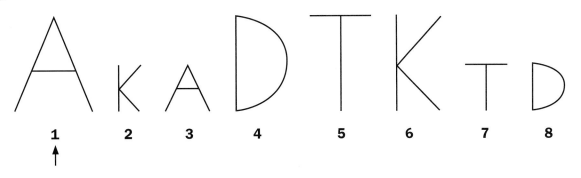

1   2   3   4   5   6   7   8

Outline Diagram

Object 1 could be described by using
_____ .

The only remaining object is _____ .

A **Write the part that is shown and finish the sentence with a good ending.**

1. I need to know why ▓▓▓▓▓▓▓▓▓▓▓▓▓▓▓ .

2. The three birds took off when ▓▓▓▓▓▓▓▓▓▓▓▓▓▓▓▓▓ .

3. The three birds landed where ▓▓▓▓▓▓▓▓▓▓▓▓▓▓▓ .

B **Write an informative article about a foreign country.**

Topics

Physical Features
Products
Ethnic Groups and Languages
Religions
History
Interesting Places to Visit

C ## PRESENT A REPORT

Check SC: Did the presenter speak clearly at a good pace?

Check O: Was the report organized with a clear introduction, followed by each recommendation, and a conclusion?

Check D: Did the report include appropriate facts and relevant details to explain each recommendation?

Check VA: Did the presenter use pictures, videos, or audio recordings to illustrate some of the main points?

▨ **SC**   ▨ **O**   ▨ **D**   ▨ **VA**

INDEPENDENT WORK

D **Follow the instructions to write a description about the arrowed object.**

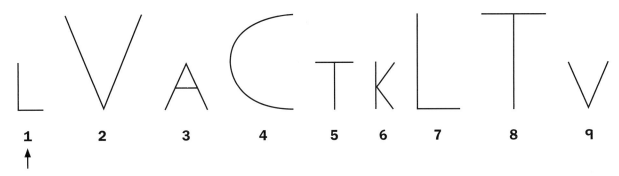

1. Write the sentence that rules out only objects 3, 4, and 6.
2. Write the sentence that rules out only objects 2, 7, and 8.
3. Write the sentence that rules out only object 9.
4. Write the sentence that rules out only object 5.

END OF LESSON 131

A Complete each sentence by adding parts that tell when, why, or where.

1. Nobody can understand why _____.

2. I found the hammer where _____.

3. She left the house when _____.

B INFORMATIVE TEXT

Title

Heading 1
Paragraphs about heading 1

Heading 2
Paragraphs about heading 2

Heading 3
Paragraphs about heading 3

C Write an informative article about a foreign country.

Topics

Physical Features
Products
Ethnic Groups and Languages
Religions
History
Interesting Places to Visit

Check I: In the first paragraph, did you introduce your topic with a general statement?

Check TS: Did you end the first paragraph with a theme sentence that briefly lists the things you're going to write about?

Check RI: Did you group related information together in paragraphs?

Check VA: Did your visual or audio materials illustrate something important?

Check CS: Did you write sentences that are complete and clear?

Check C: Did the last paragraph provide a conclusion?

Check S: Did you list your sources?

■ **I**   ■ **TS**   ■ **RI**   ■ **VA**   ■ **CS**   ■ **C**   ■ **S**

PRESENT A REPORT

Check SC: Did the presenter speak clearly at a good pace?

Check O: Was the report organized with a clear introduction, followed by each recommendation, and a conclusion?

Check D: Did the report include appropriate facts and relevant details to explain each recommendation?

Check VA: Did the presenter use pictures, videos, or audio recordings to illustrate some of the main points?

■ **SC**   ■ **O**   ■ **D**   ■ **VA**

INDEPENDENT WORK

E **Rewrite the second sentence in each item. Add transitional words or phrases to connect the two events in each item.**

1. Tia and Mia brought a new bloodhound home.
   ▓▓▓▓▓ The bloodhound slept with his nose in their shoes.

2. Koko, the cat, loved to eat the butter.
   ▓▓▓▓▓ Mia put the butter under a bowl.

3. Sid planted seeds in the garden.
   ▓▓▓▓▓ Hardly any seeds sprouted.

4. Pina talked all the time.
   ▓▓▓▓▓ Mina left the room.

END OF LESSON 132

A **Write an informative article about a <u>foreign</u> country.**

Team Tasks (no more than 4 minutes for each team member)

1. Make suggestions to improve each member's part of the report.
2. Circle one part of each member's report that needs more details.

Roles	Job Description
Team leader	Call on team members to present their topic to the team and to make suggestions for improving passages.
Time Keeper	Tell the team when 4 minutes is up.
Team Member	Listen and give feedback. Circle the part in your report that needs more detail.

Topics

Physical Features
Products
Ethnic Groups and Languages
Religions
History
Interesting Places to Visit

Check I: In the first paragraph, did you introduce your topic with a general statement?

Check TS: Did you end the first paragraph with a theme sentence that briefly lists the things you're going to write about?

Check RI: Did you group related information together in paragraphs?

Check VA: Did your visual or audio materials illustrate something important?

Check CS: Did you write sentences that are complete and clear?

Check C: Did the last paragraph provide a conclusion?

Check S: Did you list sources?

☐ **I**   ☐ **TS**   ☐ **RI**   ☐ **VA**   ☐ **CS**   ☐ **C**   ☐ **S**

B PRESENT A REPORT

Check SC: Did the presenter speak clearly at a good pace?

Check O: Was the report organized with a clear introduction, followed by each recommendation, and a conclusion?

Check D: Did the report include appropriate facts and relevant details to explain each recommendation?

Check VA: Did the presenter use pictures, videos, or audio recordings to illustrate some of the main points?

☐ SC   ☐ O   ☐ D   ☐ VA

END OF LESSON 133

A **Write an informative article about a <u>foreign</u> country.**

Team Tasks

1. Make improvements and publish it in final form, either by rewriting a clean copy or typing it in a computer.
2. Organize the topics into a final report. Write the title above the first topic.
3. List the sources at the end of the final report.

Roles	Job Description
Team leader	Call on team members to present their topics to the team and to make suggestions for improving passages.
Time Keeper	Tell the team when time is up.
Source lister	Write the list of sources for the passage.
Errand monitor	Get documents or other resources the group needs for completing the task.

Topics

Physical Features
Products
Ethnic Groups and Languages
Religions
History
Interesting Places to Visit

Check I: In the first paragraph, did you introduce your topic with a general statement?

Check TS: Did you end the first paragraph with a theme sentence that briefly lists the things you're going to write about?

Check RI: Did you group related information together in paragraphs?

Check VA: Did your visual or audio materials illustrate something important?

Check CS: Did you write sentences that are complete and clear?

Check C: Did the last paragraph provide a conclusion?

Check S: Did you list sources?

■ **I**   ■ **TS**   ■ **RI**   ■ **VA**   ■ **CS**   ■ **C**   ■ **S**

B PRESENT A REPORT

Check SC: Did the presenter speak clearly at a good pace?

Check O: Was the report organized with a clear introduction, followed by each recommendation, and a conclusion?

Check D: Did the report include appropriate facts and relevant details to explain each recommendation?

Check VA: Did the presenter use pictures, videos, or audio recordings to illustrate some of the main points?

☐ SC   ☐ O   ☐ D   ☐ VA

END OF LESSON 134

A NARRATIVE WRITING

Stories have more than one event. Here are the events in the story of the three little pigs.

1. The pig built his house of straw.
2. The wolf blew it down.
3. The pig built his next house of sticks.
4. The wolf blew it down.
5. The pig built his next house of bricks with a chimney.
6. The pig put a boiling pot of water in the fireplace under the chimney.
7. The wolf couldn't blow the house down.
8. The wolf went into the house through the chimney and ended up in the pot of boiling water.

Team Tasks

Make a list of possible events for a story.

Story beginning:

Tembi woke from a long sleep. Nothing she saw around her was familiar.

Roles	Job Description
Team leader	Call on group members one at a time to provide ideas for events.
Recorder	List the events.
Presenter	Present the list to the class.

Check PS: Did your story start with a problem situation that introduces the characters?

Check ES: Did you include events that unfold naturally?

Check T: Did you use transitional words and phrases to connect events?

Check D: Did you provide details that show how your characters responded to the events?

Check QM: Did you include quotes and punctuate them correctly?

Check E: Was the problem over at the end of the story?

■ PS   ■ ES   ■ T   ■ D   ■ QM   ■ E

B PRESENT A REPORT

Check SC: Did the presenter speak clearly at a good pace?

Check O: Was the report organized with related information grouped together?

Check D: Did the report include appropriate facts and relevant details?

Check VA: Did the pictures, videos, or audio recordings illustrate something important?

☐ **SC**   ☐ **O**   ☐ **D**   ☐ **VA**

INDEPENDENT WORK

C Rewrite the second sentence in each item. Add transitional words or phrases to connect the two events.

1. The buses were delayed by the icy roads.
   ▨ I was late to school.

2. Peter spent all day painting the porch.
   ▨ He painted the kitchen.

3. I flew my model airplane in the park.
   ▨ I ate mom's macaroni and cheese for dinner.

4. Raul was walking home from school.
   ▨ It started to rain.

A PRESENT A REPORT

Check SC: Did the presenter speak clearly at a good pace?

Check O: Was the report organized with related information grouped together?

Check D: Did the report include appropriate facts and relevant details?

Check VA: Did the pictures, videos, or audio recordings illustrate something important?

☐ SC   ☐ O   ☐ D   ☐ VA

B Revise and edit stories.

Check PS: Did your story start with a problem situation that introduces characters?

Check ES: Did you include events that unfold naturally?

Check T: Did you use transitional words and phrases to connect events?

Check D: Did you provide details that show how your characters responded to the events?

Check QM: Did you include quotes and punctuate them correctly?

Check E: Was the problem over at the end of the story?

☐ PS   ☐ ES   ☐ T   ☐ D   ☐ QM   ☐ E

END OF LESSON 136

A PRESENT A REPORT

Check SC: Did the presenter speak clearly at a good pace?

Check O: Was the report organized with related information grouped together?

Check D: Did the report include appropriate facts and relevant details?

Check VA: Did the pictures, videos, or audio recordings illustrate something important?

☐ SC ☐ O ☐ D ☐ VA

END OF LESSON 137

A **PRESENT A REPORT**

Check SC: Did the presenter speak clearly at a good pace?

Check O: Was the report organized with related information grouped together?

Check D: Did the report include appropriate facts and relevant details?

Check VA: Did the pictures, videos, or audio recordings illustrate something important?

☐ SC ☐ O ☐ D ☐ VA

B **Revise and edit and publish stories.**

Check PS: Did your story start with a problem situation that introduces characters?

Check ES: Did you include events that unfold naturally?

Check T: Did you use transitional words and phrases to connect events?

Check D: Did you provide details that show how your characters responded to the events?

Check QM: Did you include quotes and punctuate them correctly?

Check E: Was the problem over at the end of the story?

☐ PS ☐ ES ☐ T ☐ D ☐ QM ☐ E

C **PRESENT A REPORT**

Check SC: Did the presenter speak clearly at a good pace?

Check SE: Did the story start with a problem situation that resulted in an interesting sequence of events that unfolded naturally?

Check D: Did the story have detailed descriptions that showed how characters responded to events?

Check E: Did the story have a good ending?

☐ SC ☐ SE ☐ D ☐ E

END OF LESSON 138

A PRESENT A REPORT

Check SC: Did the presenter speak clearly at a good pace?

Check O: Was the report organized with related information grouped together?

Check D: Did the report include appropriate facts and relevant details?

Check VA: Did the pictures, videos, or audio recordings illustrate something important?

☐ SC   ☐ O   ☐ D   ☐ VA

B Write a story about something you experienced.

1. Make a list of events.
2. Write your story.

Check PS: Did your story start with a problem situation that introduces characters / narrator?

Check ES: Did you include events that unfold naturally?

Check T: Did you use transitional words and phrases to connect events?

Check D: Did you provide details that show how your characters responded to the events?

Check QM: Did you include quotes and punctuate them correctly?

Check E: Was the problem over at the end of the story?

☐ PS   ☐ ES   ☐ T   ☐ D   ☐ QM   ☐ E

C PRESENT A REPORT

Check SC: Did the presenter speak clearly at a good pace?

Check SE: Did the story start with a problem situation that resulted in an interesting sequence of events that unfolded naturally?

Check D: Did the story have detailed descriptions that showed how characters responded to events?

Check E: Did the story have a good ending?

☐ SC   ☐ SE   ☐ D   ☐ E

END OF LESSON 139

A PRESENT A REPORT

Check SC: Did the presenter speak clearly at a good pace?

Check O: Was the report organized with related information grouped together?

Check D: Did the report include appropriate facts and relevant details?

Check VA: Did the pictures, videos, or audio recordings illustrate something important?

■ SC   ■ O   ■ D   ■ VA

B Write a story about something you experienced.

1. Make a list of events.
2. Write your story.

Check PS: Did your story start with a problem situation that introduces characters / narrator?

Check ES: Did you include events that unfold naturally?

Check T: Did you use transitional words and phrases to connect events?

Check D: Did you provide details that show how your characters responded to the events?

Check QM: Did you include quotes and punctuate them correctly?

Check E: Was the problem over at the end of the story?

■ PS   ■ ES   ■ T   ■ D   ■ QM   ■ E

C PRESENT A REPORT

Check SC: Did the presenter speak clearly at a good pace?

Check SE: Did the story start with a problem situation that resulted in an interesting sequence of events that unfolded naturally?

Check D: Did the story have detailed descriptions that showed how characters responded to events?

Check E: Did the story have a good ending?

■ SC   ■ SE   ■ D   ■ E

END OF LESSON 140

Contractions

I am	I'm
I have	I've
I will	I'll
I would	I'd
you are	you're
you have	you've
you will	you'll
you would	you'd
he is	he's
he will	he'll
he would	he'd
she is	she's
she will	she'll
she had	she'd
it is	it's

we are	we're
we will	we'll
we have	we've
we would	we'd
they are	they're
they have	they've
they would ...	they'd
they had	they'd
they will	they'll
here is	here's
that is	that's
there is	there's
what is	what's
where is	where's
who is	who's
who will	who'll
let us	let's

are not	aren't
does not	doesn't
do not	don't
has not	hasn't
have not	haven't
is not	isn't
should not	shouldn't
was not	wasn't
were not	weren't
would not	wouldn't

cannot	can't
will not	won't

Dictionary

A

adapt   a•dapt
Verb

Adjust to new conditions, make suitable for a new use or purpose

"Hospitals have to continually adapt for modern medical practice."

Synonyms: modify, alter, change, adjust, convert, conform, redesign, revamp, redo, accomdate

altercate   al•ter•cate
Verb

Argue noisily.

"The passenger altercated with the conductor on the train."

Synonyms: quarrel, argue, squabble, fight, blowup

ambiguous   am•big•u•ous
Adjective

Open to more than one interpretation; having a double meaning.

"The question is quite ambiguous."

Synonyms: unclear, inexact, vague, uncertain

ambulate   am•bu•late
Verb

Walk, move about.

arduous   ar•du•ous
Adjective

Hard, difficult.

"Climbing the mountain was an arduous hike."

Synonyms: difficult, hard, laborious, burdensome, strenuous, tiring

C

cajole   ca•jole
Verb

Persuade someone to do something by coaxing or flattery.

"He hoped to cajole her into selling the house."

Synonyms: coax, talk into, persuade, flatter

categorical   cat•e•gor•ic•al
Adjective

Complete, absolute, definite, out-and-out, total.

cerebration   cer•e•bra•tion
Noun

Thought, the working of the brain.

"After hours of cerebration, Margie came up with a clever plan."

Synonyms: thought, analysis, consideration, problem solving

circuitous   cir•cu•i•tous
Adjective

Longer than the most direct way.

"The canal followed a circuitous route."

Synonyms: roundabout, indirect, winding, meandering, complicated.

concatenate   con•cat•e•nate
Verb

Link things together in a chain or series.

"You can concatenate parts of a story to make a whole story."

conceal   con•ceal
Verb

Hide, disguise, keep from sight.

"The sand dunes concealed the distant sea."

Synonyms: hide, disguise, mask, veil, cover, shroud.

condescending   con•de•scend•ing
Adjective

Act in a superior manner.

"Condescending people act as if they are better than others."

Synonyms: snobbish, superior, lofty, haughty, belittling.

D

delineate   de•lin•e•ate
Verb

Describe, specify.

disconcerting   dis•con•cer•ting
Adjective

Upsetting, disturbing, alarming, troubling.

 E

equipollent   e•qui•pol•lent
Adjective

Equal, the same, comparable.

expunge   ex•punge
Verb

Destroy or remove completely.

"I cannot expunge that moment from my memory."

Synonyms: get rid of, kill, destroy, remove, erase, wipe out, rub out, eradicate

 I

inundate   in•un•date
Verb

1. **flood.**

   "The islands may be the first to be inundated as sea levels rise."

   Synonyms: flood, deluge, overrun, swamp, drown, engulf

2. **overwhelm**

   (someone) with things or people to deal with.

   "We've been inundated with complaints from listeners.

   Synonyms: overwhelm, overrun, overload, bog down, swamp, bombard, glut

inactive   in•ac•tive

Adjective

Not doing anything; not operating.

incorrect   in•cor•rect

Adjective

Not accurate, not right.

ineffective   in•ef•fec•tive

Adjective

Not able to accomplish something.

insane   in•sane

Adjective

Mentally ill.

M

miniscule   min•is•cule

Adjective

Tiny, small.

"A miniscule amount of rain fell."

Synonyms: tiny, microcopic

monotonous   mo•not•o•nous

Adjective

Dull, tedious, repetitious, boring, lacking in variety and interest.

"He quotes monotonous statistics all the time."

Synonyms: boring, dull, uninteresting, unexciting, wearisome, tiresome, repetitive, unvarying, ho-hum, routine, mind-numbing.

N

nascent   na•scent

Adjective

Early, beginning, budding, developing.

P

phlegm   phlegm

Noun

Mucous, snot, especially when produced in excessive or abnormal quantities, e.g., when someone is suffering from a cold.

"He had a lot of phlegm in his lungs."

R

repudiate   re•pu•di•ate

Verb

Deny, contradict.

S

stevedore   ste•ve•dore

Noun

A person employed, or a contractor engaged, at a dock to load and unload cargo from ships.

"The stevedore worked for 15 hours without taking more than a ten-minute break."

succinct   suc•cinct

Adjective

Brief, short.

trivia   triv•i•a
Noun (plural)

Details, considerations, minor details, petty detail.

"We fill our days with meaningless trivia."

Synonyms: trifles, details, insignifcance.

unhelpful   un•help•ful
Adjective

Opposite of helpful; not assisting.

unpopular   un•pop•u•lar
Adjective

Opposite of popular; not liked.

unseen   un•seen
Adjective

Opposite of seen; not visible.

Outline Diagrams

Convey Ideas Precisely, Choose Words

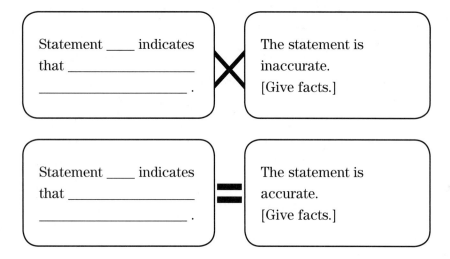

Write Informative Text

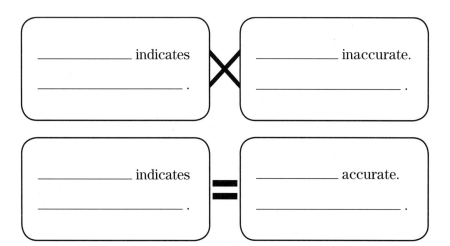

Support with Facts and Link Ideas

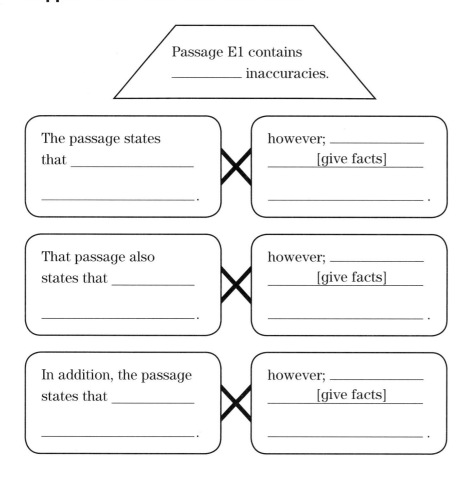

Passage E1 contains _____ inaccuracies.

The passage states that _____ _____.

however; _____ _____ [give facts] _____.

That passage also states that _____ _____.

however; _____ _____ [give facts] _____.

In addition, the passage states that _____ _____.

however; _____ _____ [give facts] _____.

Evaluate Discrepancies in Sources

The Clipper ad contains _____.

The ad indicates _____ _____ _____;

however, [give parallel fact] _____. The only items you'll save on are _____.

You will not _____ _____ _____.

Write Opinion Piece—Respond to Misleading and Inaccurate Claims

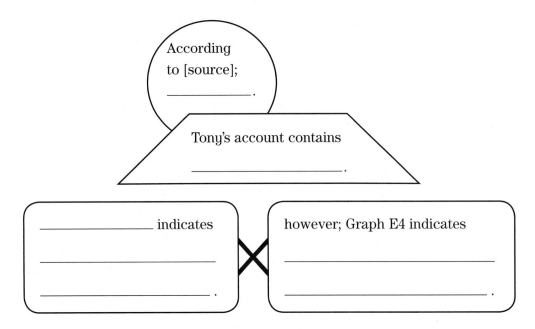

Write Opinion Piece—Respond to Misleading and Inaccurate Claims

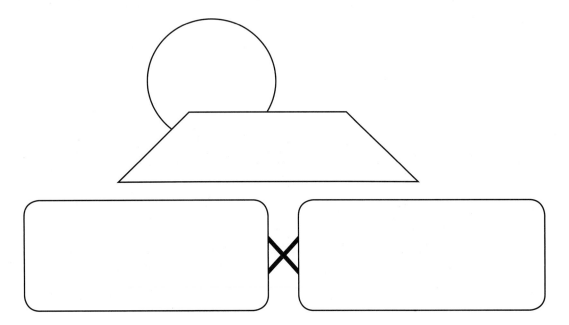

Write Opinion Piece—Respond to Misleading Impressions

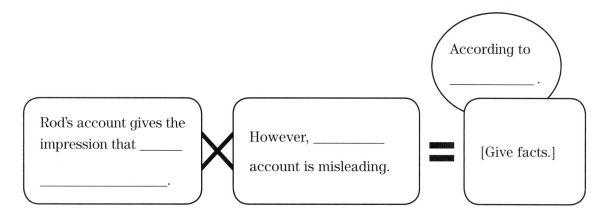

Rod's account gives the impression that _____ _____ .

However, _____ account is misleading.

According to _____ .

[Give facts.]

Write Opinion Piece—Respond to More General Conclusions

Phil concludes that _____ _____ _____ .

however, his conclusion is more general than the evidence. Evidence about [a specific category] cannot lead to a proper conclusion about [a general category].

Write Opinion Piece—Respond to More General Conclusions

however, _____ . Evidence about [a specific category] _____ [a general category].

Write Informative Text—Take Notes and Categorize Information

1. main thing

   details

Copy this outline on your lined paper:

1. tallest trees

2.

3.

Narrative Writing—Write About Real Experiences

Paragraph 1:   [Use words from the directions] occurred [tell when].
[Tell where]. [Summarize what happened to frighten you.]

Paragraph 2:   [Tell details of what happened—what you did.]
[Tell how you felt at the end.]

Draw Evidence to Support Analysis and Reflection—Draw Inferences in Literary Texts

Al would have performed better if he had followed the
coach's training program. [Compare Diego's training
and performance with Al's training and performance.]

Draw Evidence to Support Analysis and Reflection—Draw Inferences in Literary Texts

Mr. Mosely did not know important things about himself. One thing he didn't know was that
_____ . Another thing he didn't know was that
_____ .

Draw Evidence to Support Analysis and Reflection—Draw Inferences in Literary Texts

Ann did something that required courage. [Describe what Ann did.]

Draw Evidence to Support Analysis and Reflection—Draw Inferences in Literary Texts

The statement about Ann is true. [Write the true statement.] The evidence is in paragraph 2. [Write sentences that tell what happened before the quote.] The story continues: "[Copy the quote exactly.]"

Reasoning—Write About Contradictions

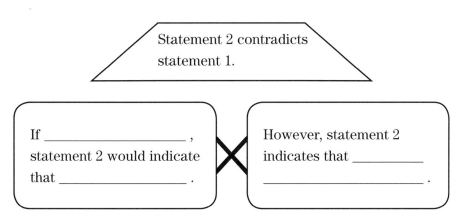

Reasoning—Write About Contradictions

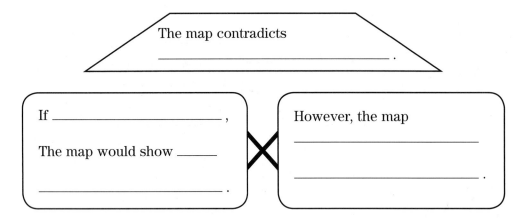

The map contradicts
_____ .

If _____ ,

The map would show _____

_____ .

However, the map

_____

_____ .

Reasoning—Write About Internal Contradictions

Teeny contradicted himself.

If _____

_____ ,

Teeny's last statement would indicate

that _____ .

However, Teeny's last statement

indicates that _____

_____ .

Reasoning—Write About Internal Contradictions

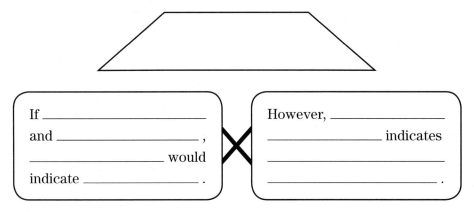

If _____

and _____ ,

_____ would

indicate _____ .

However, _____

_____ indicates

_____

_____ .

Reasoning—Write Alternative Conclusions Allowed by the Evidence

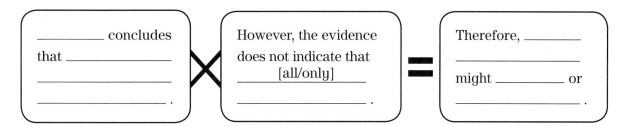

Reasoning—Write Alternative Conclusions Allowed by the Evidence

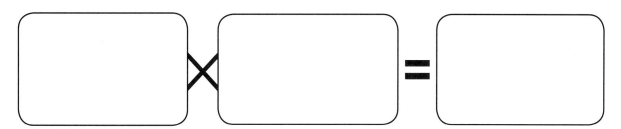

Use Precise Language—Evaluate Precision of Language

Object 1 could be described by using only sentence _____ and sentence _____ .

Sentence _____ rules out objects _____ and _____ .

Sentence _____ _____ _____ .

Explanatory Text—Use Clues to Rule Out Possibilities

The mystery object is _____ .

Clue A rules out _____ .
possibilities. They are
_____ , _____ , and _____ .

The only remaining possibility is _____ .

Punctuation—Use Colon and Semicolon

The most practical route is
_____
_____ .

=

That route has these

advantages: it _____

_____ ; it _____ .

Explanatory Text—Use Requirements to Rule Out Options

Paragraph 1

_____ houses meet the Hunter family's requirements.

Those houses are located at _____ .

Requirement _____ rules out the house located at _____ . That house _____ .

Requirement _____

_____

_____

_____ .

Paragraph 2

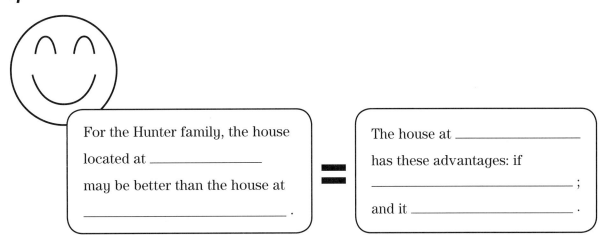

For the Hunter family, the house located at _____ may be better than the house at _____ .

=

The house at _____ has these advantages: if _____ ; and it _____ .

Evaluate Ideas—Write Opinion About Plans

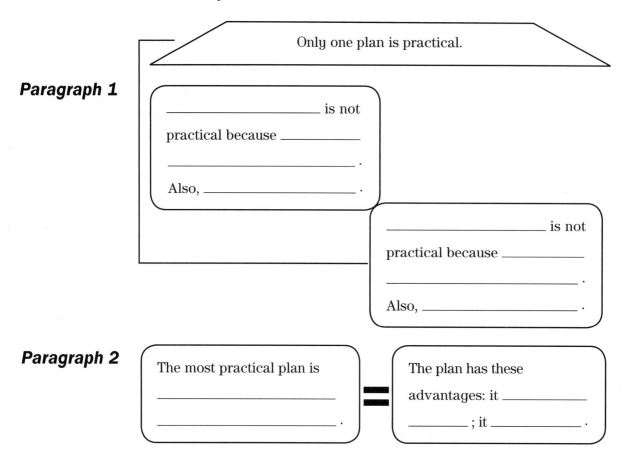

Paragraph 1

Only one plan is practical.

_____ is not practical because _____ .

Also, _____ .

_____ is not practical because _____ .

Also, _____ .

Paragraph 2

The most practical plan is _____ .

=

The plan has these advantages: it _____ ; it _____ .

Research Report—Write Advice on How to Achieve a Goal

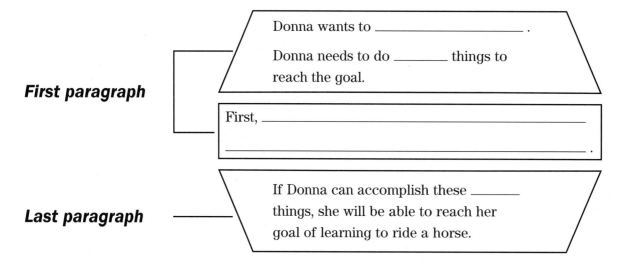

First paragraph

Donna wants to _____ .

Donna needs to do _____ things to reach the goal.

First, _____ .

Last paragraph

If Donna can accomplish these _____ things, she will be able to reach her goal of learning to ride a horse.

Informative Text—Write an Informative Article

1. Paragraph 1 gives the most general description. It ends with the theme sentence. The theme sentence tells what comes next. This theme sentence lists the three things the next three paragraphs discuss in detail.

2. Each paragraph groups related information together. Paragraph 2 is about the first recommended experience.

3. Paragraph 3 is about the second experience.

4. Paragraph 4 is about the third experience.

5. The last paragraph is the conclusion. You can use the conclusion to highlight something in all three experiences you recommend.

Reference Section
Facts

birds — Birds, class Aves, are warm-blooded, egg-laying animals with a backbone. Birds are covered with FEATHERS and have wings. A few families of birds (such as OSTRICHES, EMUS, and RHEAS) and some species of otherwise flying families (for example, some GREBES, RAILS, and CORMORANTS) cannot fly. Others (such as PENGUINS) have become adapted to flying in water, but not in air.

bicycle — two-wheeled, motorless vehicle invented in 1813.

bones — (See *skeleton.*)

Chile — (See *South America.*)

Columbus — Columbus was a European who landed in America in 1492.

corn — Corn is an important farm crop. Corn is a plant of the grass family. The plant possesses both male and female flowers. The male flowers are in the tassel at the top of the stalk, and the female flowers become the cob, at a joint of the stalk. Among the world's four most important crops (the others are wheat, rice, and potatoes), corn is native to America. The United States produces over 40 percent of the world's corn. Countries with large areas devoted to corn include the United States, China, Brazil, Mexico, Argentina, Romania, France, India, and South Africa.

fowl — The term is usually used with an adjective, for example, wild fowl or water fowl. If the term is used without an adjective, it means birds that are raised for food or it means bird meat.

mammals — The largest mammal is the blue whale. Seals, dolphins, otters, walruses, and whales are mammals that live in the ocean.

mountains — The tallest mountain in the world is Mt. Everest, which is 29,035 feet high (almost $5\frac{1}{2}$ miles).

Mountains	Feet	Meters	Location
Everest	29,035	8,850	Nepal-Tibet
K2	28,251	8,611	Kashmir
Kanchenjunga	28,169	8,586	Nepal-Sikkim
Lhotse 1	27,940	8,516	Nepal-Tibet
Makalu 1	27,766	8,463	Nepal-Tibet

redwood forests — The redwood tree is the earth's tallest tree. The giant redwood forests of northern California were so impressive that the United States created national parks to preserve them. A car can drive through a tunnel made in a giant redwood tree. Redwood trees grow along the west coast of the United States, from southern Oregon to central California.

skeleton — The adult human skeleton is comprised of 206 individual bones. The three main functions of the skeletal system are protection, motion, and support. The following diagram shows some of the important bones in the skeleton.

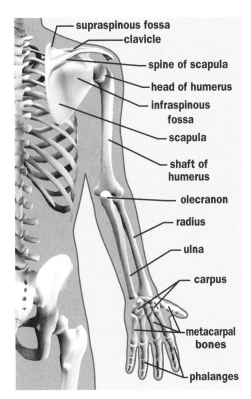

South America —

	Source Data	
Country	**Population as of 2016**	**Area in Square Miles**
Argentina	43,847,277	1,073,518
Bolivia	10,888,402	424,164
Brazil	209,567,920	3,287,597
Chile	18,131,850	291,930
Colombia	48,654,392	440,831
Ecuador	16,385,450	109,483
French Guiana	275,688	32,253
Guyana	770,610	83,000
Paraguay	6,725,430	157,048
Peru	31,774,225	496,225
Suriname	547,610	63,251
Uruguay	3,444,071	68,037
Venezuela	31,815,855	353,841
Total	424,465,186	6,881,178

Suriname — (See *South America*.)

water — Water freezes at 32° Fahrenheit (0° Celsius) and boils at 212° Fahrenheit (100° Celsius).

wheat — Wheat is second only to rice in importance as a world food source. Wheat is grown on more of the world's acreage than any other food.

year — 365 days make a year, except leap year (every fourth year). One leap year has 366 days, with February 29 occurring every four years.

Resources

Thursday, 7:45 P.M., at 1230 Devine Street.

Don and Donna Jackson claim that a dog owned by Rod Vernon dug a hole in their backyard. Rod Vernon did not deny that the dog named Herman had been let out and may have dug a hole. The hole measures 12 feet wide and 5 feet deep. There was a pile of dirt on one side that was over 6 feet high.

ENGINEER'S REPORT

The bridge would have to be at least 30 feet high, 8 feet wide, and 200 feet long. The materials would cost around $200,000. The steel beams would be the most expensive items. Installing the bridge would cost another $300,000 in labor and equipment.

A LETTER THAT LISA'S SISTER WROTE TO A FRIEND:

My sister can be a real pain. She pestered my parents to give her a birthday party. So they finally gave in. Lisa sent out the invitations. Then, a couple of days before the party, my mother was talking to Lisa about the cake. Lisa said that we would need ten cakes.

My mother almost fell over. "Ten cakes?" she screamed. "How many people did you invite to the party?"

Lisa told her, "One hundred."

So now Lisa can't understand why our parents are mad at her.

Work and Goals
by Harry Smith

1 The team's new track coach had a long talk with each member of the team. Al was the third member that Coach Ricker talked to. He told Al, "You've got some talent . . . but so do a lot of others."

2 He then went into a long lecture on what it takes to become competitive. The coach must have used the word *competitive* twenty times in his speech.

3 Al didn't really believe what the coach said. He knew he had talent. He thought that he could win the regional cross-country meet if he simply continued to train the way he had been training. He didn't do all the things that the coach talked about—none of the wind sprints, the weight training, the dieting, and what the coach called serious hill climbing. Al believed that he could keep on improving if he just ran the two-mile course one time during the week and did one longer run on the weekend, but not a run that involved "serious hill climbing."

4 Al told his teammate, Diego, about his talk with Coach Ricker. Diego said, "I think he's probably right. You have to make sacrifices if you want to excel."

5 Al didn't say anything, but he had a lot of thoughts. Most of them had to do with how ridiculous Diego was. Al had beaten Diego in every distance event. Al was tempted to say, "You could follow his training procedures all year long and I'd still beat you in one mile, two miles, or in cross country." But all Al said was, "So you're going to buy into his program?"

6 "Yeah."

7 The weather was perfect for the regional meet, cool but not cold, light wind, and some clouds. Al felt good. "I'm ready," he told Diego before the contest. Al checked his watch. He had a pretty good idea of where he should be after 2,000 meters and 4,000 meters. His times had improved over the season.

8 And they were even a little better than Al had planned. He was shooting for a time of 15 minutes and 55 seconds to complete the course. At 4,000 meters of the race, Al was almost 10 seconds ahead of the mark. But when there were less than 500 meters to the end of the course, Diego pulled even with Al. Al tried to keep up with Diego, but he felt his legs getting stiff as if they were trying to move through thick syrup. Diego finished four seconds ahead of Al.

9 Coach Ricker later told them, "You both did a good job. I'm proud of you, and you should be proud of yourself. You both made the sacrifices and gave it all you had."

10 Al wasn't happy with himself because he hadn't given all he had.

Side Effects
by Margie Noll

1   Everybody who came to Oak Lane was impressed by the beautiful yards—three blocks of weedless, bright green lawns, perfectly manicured shrubs, and colorful flower gardens. The most impressive grounds surrounded the Mosely house. The yard was almost a full acre, with an incredible rose garden and a spotless lawn. Mr. Mosely was in charge of the grounds, and he spent just about all his spare time spraying, pruning, fertilizing, mowing, and watering. It was a lot of work, but the rewards were great. His neighbors envied him. People driving by would often slow down to view the vast rolling front yard and marvel over the grass.

2   There was one problem—the giant birdbath to the west of the house. Mr. Mosely and his wife loved to sit on their deck and watch the birds take baths. The problem was that fewer and fewer birds visited the birdbath. Also, during the last month, Mr. Mosely found two dead birds on the lawn—a brilliant red cardinal and a robin. Was somebody in the neighborhood poisoning them? Why was the bird population going down?

3   Mr. Mosely puzzled over these questions early one morning when he found a third dead bird, a plain little sparrow, lying there like a little statue with its wings tucked tightly against its sides and no expression on its little bird face. Mr. Mosely bent down over the dead bird and wished the bird could tell him who was responsible for this horrible evil.

4   He buried the sparrow at the north end of the rose garden. Then he continued to spray the lawn with weed killer. He ran out of weed killer a short time later and had to go to the lawn-and-garden shop to buy more. While he was there, he noticed that pest spray was on sale, at a good price. This was an excellent time to stock up. As he was loading his shopping cart, the clerk, Marty, passed by and said, "Mr. Mosely, you keep us in business with all the lawn preparation material you buy."

5   "Yes sir," Mr. Mosely said. "That's why I have the most beautiful lawn in the area. No bugs or weeds on my grounds."

6   "You're right," Marty said. "Your lawn is gorgeous."

Get Hold of Yourself
By Ana Cardona

1   This was the fifth time Ann would take the test for becoming a firefighter. This was also the last time she would be eligible to take the test. She had worked hard during the last two years, but she wasn't sure that she would be able to hold the hose when it was under pressure or carry a full-grown man down the stairs. These were the two parts of the test she had failed before—again and again. Since her last failure, she had worked hard by lifting weights and carrying heavy things up and down stairs.

2   On the day of the exam, she felt weak and sick. She said to herself, "You're just suffering from a case of nervousness—stage fright. Get hold of yourself." But about a minute later, she picked up the phone and started to dial. She felt that she was too weak to take the test. She was going to tell the committee that she had decided not to take the test.

3   Before she dialed the last four numbers, she told herself, "You've worked so hard that you can't quit now. You need to know if you can pass that test."

4   She put the phone down and decided to take the test.

5   At 4:30 that afternoon, Ann completed the test. She walked from the old building in which the test was held. Then she jumped up, shot her fist as high into the air as she could, and shouted, "Yes! Yes!" She knew that she had passed the test. She had held the hose as still as most of the men she had seen pass the test, and she had picked up Eddie, who was larger than most full-grown men, and carried him down two flights of stairs. "Yes, yes," she said to herself. "Your courage paid off."

6   Two weeks later she received her license as a city firefighter.

Personal Best
by Isabel Ramos

1 Maria did not make the District All-Star Team. She got the news on Friday. The coaches said her outside shot was not good enough for a shooting guard, and she was too slow to play point guard. She said to her mom, "I'm not too slow." Then she started to frown because she knew that they were probably right. Some players were definitely faster than she was.

2 "Honey," her mom said. "We're proud of you. You're a wonderful athlete and a very good basketball player. It's just that there are some players who are a little bit better."

3 "So you don't think I'm good enough to be an all-star?"

4 "As far as I'm concerned you'll always be an all-star, and maybe you should have made the district team, but . . . "

5 "So you don't think I'm good enough."

6 "No, I didn't say that. But you shouldn't just look at those who are a tiny bit better than you are. Look at the hundreds of girls who are nowhere near as good as you are."

7 "I don't care about them," Maria said. "I think I play as well as Cindy Ulrick, and she's on the All-Star Team."

8 "Honey, let it go. Look at what you've accomplished and be proud of it. You're one of the best players Lincoln High School has ever had. That's a great achievement."

9 "Not if I can't even make the All-Star Team."

10 Cindy Ulrick called Maria the next morning, Saturday, and told her how sad she was that Maria did not make the team. Maria had competed against Cindy since they were in the middle-school league. She liked her a lot. "Listen," Cindy said, "If you're not doing anything this morning, let's shoot some hoops."

11 "No, I don't feel . . ."

12 "Come on, Maria. It will take your mind off things."

13 After a little more coaxing, Maria agreed. Cindy picked Maria up. "Do you mind if we go to the courts across from Donner Hospital?"

14 "That's okay, but why do you want to go there?"

15 "I have to pick up my sister Beth when we're done. She's in physical therapy at the hospital."

16 Maria had met Beth once before. She was a couple years older than Cindy. She had a problem with her back and legs that made it difficult for her to walk. She couldn't do anything athletic.

17 The girls played a little One-on-One and Horse. Maria won both games, but she suspected that Cindy may have let her win. "Come on," Maria said. "You play One-on-One better than that."

18 "Hey, I was trying. You were just hot today."

19 They went into the hospital, and Maria started to feel uneasy. She hated hospitals. They took the elevator to the fourth floor, where there was a huge room with mats, machines of all kinds, weights, and lots of people.

20 Cindy spotted her sister on the far side of the room. As the girls drew near, Maria noticed that there were three people around the machine Beth was using, and they were urging her on. "Come on, Beth," a man in a wheelchair shouted. "You can do it."

21 A man on crutches with only one leg yelled, "One more. One more."

22 The girls arrived in time to see Beth finish the exercise. She was on her back, pushing a weight with her right leg. "That's five reps," the man on crutches shouted. "Five reps."

23 Beth sat up awkwardly. Her face was red, and she was beaming. "How about that?" she yelled. "I did it!" She gave the men high-fives and then noticed Cindy and Maria.

24 Beth said, "I set a personal best."

25 "Yeah?" Cindy said. "How much?"

26 "Fifteen pounds, five times."

27 Good for you." Cindy high-fived her sister.

28 Then she helped her sister stand up.

29 Maria thought to herself, "15 pounds? I could press twice that much with one arm. If she can't do any more than that with one leg . . . " Maria turned away. She could hear the sisters talking.

30 "Well, what are we going to do to celebrate?" Cindy asked.

31 "I don't know about you, but I'm having some cake," Beth answered.

32 Later that afternoon, Maria told her mother that she was right to say that morning that Maria should be grateful for the gifts that Maria has. She gave her mom a hug.

Thesaurus

A

ambiguous

Synonyms: *vague, inexact, uncertain, unclear*

Antonyms: *clear, precise, certain*

B

big

Synonyms: *large, huge, gigantic, enormous*

Antonyms: *small, tiny, puny, insignificant*

bright

Synonyms: *blazing, brilliant, dazzling, shining, glowing, shimmering, vivid, radiant*

Antonyms: *dull, dark, drab*

C

circuitous

Synonyms: *roundabout, indirect, winding, meandering, complicated*

Antonyms: *direct, straight, straightforward*

conducive

Synonyms: *helpful, useful, favorable for*

Antonyms: *unfavorable for, useless, worthless*

D

derogatory

Synonyms: *offensive, uncomplimentary, insulting, belittling*

Antonyms: *encouraging, complimentrary, appreciating, flattering*

E

elaborate

Synonyms: *detailed, embellished, fancy, garnished, imposing, complicated*

Antonyms: *simple, uncultured, unrefined, plain, unsophisticated*

elated

Synonyms: *delighted, ecstatic, enchanted, excited, joyful*

Antonyms: *depressed, disappointed, miserable, sorrowful, troubled*

equipollent

Synonyms: *equal, the same, comparable, a match for*

Antonyms: *different, unlike, unequal*

find

Synonyms: *identify, discover, locate, detect*

Antonyms: *miss, overlook, pass over*

good looking

Synonyms: *pretty, lovely, handsome, beautiful*

Antonyms: *homely, repellent, unattractive, ugly*

happy

Synonyms: *pleased, delighted, ecstatic, joyful, cheerful*

Antonyms: *sad, depressed, morose, unhappy*

impressive

Synonyms: *extraordinary, notable, remarkable, grand*

Antonyms: *commonplace, insignificant, normal, ordinary, unimposing, unimpressive.*

like

Synonyms: *favor, fancy, relish, approve*

Antonyms: *deplore, despise, regret, resent, hate*

miniscule

Synonyms: *tiny, small, unimportant*

Antonyms: *huge, enormous, important*

nice

Synonyms: *attractive, agreeable, pretty, polite, kind*

Antonyms: *disagreeable, horrible, nasty, unpleasant*

silly

Synonyms: *absurd, foolish, crazy, ridiculous*

Antonyms: *mature, serious, responsible, intelligent, reasonable*

smart

Synonyms: *intelligent, astute, bright, sharp*

Antonyms: *unintelligent, ignorant, unwise, foolish*

tired

Synonyms: *weary, exhausted, drained, fatigued, overworked, sleepy*

Antonyms: *energized, invigorated, fired up, refreshed, rested*

wish for

Synonyms: *long for, yearn for, desire, crave, fancy*

Antonyms: *content, pleased, satisfied*

Verb-Noun List

VERB	NOUN	VERB	NOUN
adapt	adaptation	decorate	decoration
adjust	adjustment	dedicate	dedication
agree	agreement	deduct	deduction
altercate	altercation	demonstrate	demonstration
apply	application	describe	description
appoint	appointment	destroy	destruction
argue	argument	develop	development
arrange	arrangement	differ	difference
assert	assertion	direct	direction
assign	assignment	disagree	disagreement
assist	assistance	discover	discovery
associate	association	distract	distraction
assume	assumption	disturb	disturbance
attach	attachment	divide	division
attend	attendance	educate	education
behave	behavior	elevate	elevation
believe	belief	entertain	entertainment
bite	bite	erase	erasure
choose	choice	erode	erosion
collect	collection	erupt	eruption
collide	collision	establish	establishment
communicate	communication	estimate	estimation
compare	comparison	evacuate	evacuation
compete	competition	evaporate	evaporation
complain	complaint	evolve	evolution
compose	composition	exaggerate	exaggeration
conclude	conclusion	examine	examination
confess	confession	except	exception
confuse	confusion	excite	excitement
connect	connection	exclaim	exclamation
conserve	conservation	exclude	exclusion
construct	construction	exhibit	exhibition
contradict	contradiction	exist	existence
contribute	contribution	expand	expansion
converse	conversation	expect	expectation
cooperate	cooperation	explain	explanation
criticize	criticism	explode	explosion
declare	declaration	explore	exploration

VERB	NOUN	VERB	NOUN
extend	extension	inspire	inspiration
fail	failure	install	installment/installation
fascinate	fascination	instruct	instruction
fertilize	fertilization	interfere	interference
flatter	flattery	interpret	interpretation
fulfill	fulfillment	interrogate	interrogation
fuse	fusion	interrupt	interruption
gather	gathering	introduce	introduction
glorify	glorification	invade	invasion
graduate	graduation	invest	investment
gravitate	gravitation	invite	invitation
grow	growth	involve	involvement
happen	happening	jeopardize	jeopardy
harass	harassment	join	joint
harmonize	harmony	judge	judgment
hate	hatred	kindle	kindling
hesitate	hesitation	locate	location
horrify	horror	marry	marriage
hypnotize	hypnotism	object	objection
identify	identification	observe	observation
ignore	ignorance	perform	performance
illuminate	illumination	practice	practice
illustrate	illustration	prepare	preparation
imagine	imagination	propose	proposal
impede	impediment	punctuate	punctuation
impress	impression	relate	relation
improve	improvement	remind	reminder
improvise	improvisation	request	request
include	inclusion	require	requirement
indent	indentation	rotate	rotation
indicate	indication	sing	song
induct	induction	state	statement
infect	infection	study	study/studying
infer	inference	summarize	summary
inherit	inheritance	theorize	theory
injure	injury	transform	transformation
inquire	inquiry	vacate	vacation
insist	insistence	vaccinate	vaccination
inspect	inspection	warn	warning